Dr Sue Chadwick is a senior associate with Birketts LLP, has more than 20 years experience and a PhD in planning law. As well as working for a range of County and District authorities, two London Boroughs, and a number of years at Herbert Smith Freehills she has taught planning law and policy at Cambridge University. She also has direct practical experience of the process from her membership of the Isle of Dogs Planning Forum.

In My Backyard!

A Practical Guide to Neighbourhood Plans

In My Backyard!
A Practical Guide to Neighbourhood Plans

Dr Sue Chadwick
Solicitor

Law Brief Publishing

Published 2018 by Law Brief Publishing, an imprint of Law Brief Publishing Ltd
30 The Parks
Minehead
Somerset
TA24 8BT

www.lawbriefpublishing.com

Paperback: 978-1-911035-74-9

PREFACE

Planning law has been my professional preoccupation for more than 30 years now. At first, neighbourhood planning was simply another – albeit unusual – addition to the range of issues I needed to know about as part of that practice. Moving to London – and becoming a Committee Member of the Isle of Dogs Neighbourhood Planning Forum – made neighbourhood planning a personal as well as a professional concern.

Engaging with this new element of the planning system as a resident as well as a solicitor – and helping the other Forum members to negotiate their way round the process – brought home just how difficult it can be to bring a neighbourhood plan forward in compliance with all of the legal requirements while preserving the essence of its policies in a way that still serves the local community.

This book is aimed primarily at groups like our Forum, so that they have access to a basic guide to the process. It will also be useful to officers and Members of local authorities dealing with the issue for the first time, and will be a sound starting point for other lawyers interested in this fascinating element of the English planning system. The law and policies referred to are accurate as at the end of May 2018.

This book would not have come about at all without the Isle of Dogs Neighbourhood Planning Forum so it is dedicated primarily to Richard, Andrew and all the other committee members. It would not have been written so quickly without the enduring support and tolerance of my colleagues at Birketts LLP. It is dedicated to them all.

Dr Sue Chadwick
May 2018

CONTENTS

PART ONE

Introduction

On 18th November 2010 Greg Clark, the then Shadow Secretary of State for Energy and Climate Change in October 2008, gave a speech to Localis, an independent, think tank promoting neo-localist ideas.[1] Mr Clark talked about the need to "reboot planning to meet the needs of the 21st century" and went on to assert that "The principle is simple. Local people come together and agree, "this is what we want our area to look like. Here is where we want the new homes to go and how we want them designed; here is where we want new shops and offices; here are the green spaces we want to protect."

On 13th December 2010 Eric Pickles, then Secretary of State for Communities and Local Government, introduced the Localism Bill to Parliament[2], claiming that it would function as the foundation of the Coalition's vision of a new, 'big society… radically transforming the relationships between central government, local government, communities and individuals'. The Bill included proposals for a new element of the planning system – Neighbourhood Planning – comprising:

- A new category of development order – the Community Right to Build – enabling permission to be granted in certain places for certain types of development;

---

1 https://www.gov.uk/government/speeches/better-planning-from-principle-to-practice

2 http://hansard.parliament.uk/commons/2010-12-13/debates/10121320000015/LocalismBill

- A new kind of development plan – the Neighbourhood Development Plan ("NDP"); made by communities rather than local authorities.

Although Mr Pickles described the proposals as a "triumph for democracy over bureaucracy"[3] this statement was not supported by the complex web of laws and policies that are currently in place to regulate the process of making and adopting a neighbourhood plan.

The Localism Act introduces selective changes to existing planning Acts: the Town and Country Planning Act 1990 ("the 1990 Act") and the Planning and Compulsory Purchase Act 2004 ("the 2004 Act") and delegated legislation, principally The Neighbourhood Planning (General) Regulations 2012[4] ("the 2012 Regulations") and the Neighbourhood Planning (Referendums) Regulations 2012[5] ("the Referendum Regulations"). Further changes have been brought in with the Housing and Planning Act 2016 and the Neighbourhood Planning Act 2017. In addition, neighbourhood planning is referred to a number of times in the 2012 National Planning Policy Framework ("the Framework") and has its own section in the government's online National Planning Policy Guidance ("the NPPG"). In *Kebbell Developments* Mr Justice Kerr agreed with the description of the current system as a "statutory thicket"[6] and it is hard to disagree.

---

3 https://publications.parliament.uk/pa/cm201011/cmhansrd/cm110117/debtext/110117-0001.htm#1101176000001

4 SI 2012/637

5 SI 2012/2031

6 Kebbell Developments Ltd, R (on the application of) v Leeds City Council & Anor [2016] EWHC 2664 (Admin)

It is a long time since any politician has mentioned the Big Society. The vote on whether or not to leave Europe revealed an increasingly divided nation and in this post-Brexit world political attention is focussed on economic survival and solving the housing crisis. . Nevertheless, neighbourhood planning is alive and well and appears to be one of the few areas of law and policy that politicians on both sides of the house see as largely positive. It has been a rare political success story for the Government, and is an enduringly popular concept with local communities. This political support has been backed up by the plans in practice. Some neighbourhood plans have been able to prevent or control local development as, if not more, effectively than the local plan.

Neighbourhood planning has been good for the lawyers too: neighbourhood plans have generated a significant amount of case law, in areas including compliance with key European Directives on Environmental Assessment and Habitats Regulations, the requirement for the plan to be 'in conformity with' the relevant local authority plan, and even whether or not plan examiners were biased. The legal and policy context is wide and complex, and the issues are significant and contentious. For the local group considering its own plan, or for the local authority charged with overseeing the development and adoption of such a plan, the prospects can be daunting.

This book is intended to provide an overview of the making, adoption, and implementation of the neighbourhood development plan. It will set out an overview of the process, and the legislation driving that process and will identify and explain the key conclusions in the relevant case law in each area. It will include, where relevant, reference to key national planning policy and guidance, and will end with a reflection on the current and future relevance of neighbourhood planning in the planning landscape.

Overview of the Neighbourhood Plan Process

Traditional development plans produced by local authorities involve the following key stages:

- Information gathering involving research and analysis on a range of economic, social and environmental subjects to provide a factual base for the plan and initial consultation with local councils and other relevant bodies.

- Publication of an Issues Paper setting out a series of strategic, general and local issues against which representations may be lodged.

- Further consultation and research before publication of the draft plan and a further consultation.

- An examination in Public which can take months, sometimes more than a year, to conclude.

- Publication of the Examiners report and adoption of the plan.

In addition, in order to show compliance with the Framework, the local authority must show that: 1) the statutory duty to cooperate contained in section 110 of the Localism Act 2011 has been taken into account and complied with and 2) that the plan meets the criteria set out in the NPPG to show that it is 'sound'. This is a long and complex process. Indeed, the difficulty of getting plans adopted was considered in the 2014 report of the House of Commons Communities and Local Government Committee[7] who described plan production as a game of 'snakes and ladders' where years of progress could be negated in the final stages of plan production with the publication of an unfavourable inspector's report.

In contrast the neighbourhood plan involves just one significant consultation stage and may be examined without any need for a public hearing. The basic process for making and adopting an NDP can be summarised as follows:

- There must be a valid qualifying body to make the plan.
- There must be a designated area to which the plan relates.
- The qualifying body begins with preparation of a draft of the plan and consults on it locally. The relevant local authority must give advice and assistance as it considers appropriate during this process. As soon as the draft plan exists, it will be a material consideration in the determination of planning applications.
- The qualifying body then submits the plan formally to the relevant local planning authority.
- If the local planning authority is satisfied that the draft plan meets certain statutory requirements it must publish the plan, consult on it publicly and then submit the draft plan for independent examination by an examiner appointed for that purpose.

7 Communities and Local Government Committee, *Operation of the National Planning Policy Framework* (HC 2014-15, 190)

- The examiner must consider whether the draft plan meets "the basic conditions" including whether or not it is appropriate to make the order having regard to national policies and advice, and whether the order is "in general conformity with" strategic policies in the development plan.

- The examiner must take into account representations made. These are generally made in writing rather than orally, but there is scope for an oral hearing in some circumstances.

- The examiner must make a report on the draft plan, with reasons, and recommendations.

- The examiner can recommend modifications where the examiner considers that they are required to secure that the draft plan meets the basic conditions. The examiner may recommend that the draft plan should be submitted to a referendum; or that it should be submitted to a referendum with specified modifications; or that it should be rejected.

- The local planning authority must consider the examiner's recommendations and reasons and decide what action to take. The authority must publish its "decision statement" if satisfied that the draft plan meets the "basic conditions".

- The only modifications the local planning authority may make to the draft plan are modifications it considers necessary to "secure that the draft [plan] meets the basic conditions.

- If the local planning authority proposes to make a decision that differs from that recommended by the examiner the authority must notify "prescribed persons" of its decision and reasons, and invite representations, or refer the issue to independent examination.

- If satisfied that the basic conditions are met the local planning authority must put the draft plan to a local referendum.

- Once held, if the referendum is in favour of making the plan, it is made.

- Once made, the NDP becomes part of the 'Development Plan for the area with equal status to other local authority policies and is taken into account as a primary consideration in all planning decisions.

As soon as neighbourhood plan is formally adopted it becomes a key element in the complex process of considering and deciding planning applications, because it becomes one of the documents that must be considered in the determination of all applications – the development plan.

PART TWO

Planning Decisions – The Development Plan

The Housing, Town Planning Act of 1909 established the founding principles of development plans and subsequent legislation has broadened their range and scope. These plans are formulated, assessed and adopted by local planning authorities and set development aspirations and constraints within which new development will evolve. They generally include a range of development management and design principles and may also matters of wider public interest such as health, amenity and infrastructure provision. As was recognised in the 2012 *Tesco Stores* case the development plan is there to be followed "unless there is good reason to depart from it"[1] and the Framework also states at paragraph 198 "where a planning application conflicts with a neighbourhood plan that has been brought into force, planning permission should not normally be granted."

Development plans are defined in Section 38 of the 2004 Act as follows:

- In London the development plan is the London Plan, the development plan documents adopted or approved and any neighbourhood plans which have been made in relation to the area.

- In the remainder of England the development plan is the development plan documents adopted or approved and any neighbourhood development plans made in relation to the area.

---

1 Tesco Stores Ltd v. Dundee City Council [2012] UKSC 13, [2012] 2 P&CR 9

- Section 38A(2) of the 2004 Act specifically included NDPs as part of the development plan, describing such plans as a document "which sets out policies in relation to the development and use of land in the whole or any part of a particular neighbourhood area specified in the plan."

The courts do not often consider the formal definition of a development plan but in *RWE Npower* Mr Justice Howell ruled that "provided a document fulfils a function which a local development document is intended to serve (as defined in section 17(3) of the 2004 Act), which is to set out the authority's policies relating to the development and use of land in its area, and provided it is adopted by the authority (as required by section 17(8)), it is a "local development document"[2]. He went on to rule that development plan documents would include development management policies, strategic plan policies, and area plans but would not include supplementary planning documents.

Neighbourhood plans are a new element in an established structure and can be distinguished from the other documents that are categorised as development plans in a number of ways. The key distinguishing factor is that they are generated from, drafted by and consulted on – at least in the initial stages – by ordinary members of a local community rather than the established local authority. In addition, the making and adoption of neighbourhood plans is governed by a completely separate legislative process.

The difficulty of getting a traditional development plan adopted is summarised above. Neighbourhood plans are not subject to any of these constraints; legal validity depends on compliance with the

2 WE Npower Renewables Ltd, R (on the application of) v Ecotricity (Next Generation) Ltd [2013] EWHC 751 (Admin)

basic conditions rather than the more detailed concept of "soundness" applied to other development plan documents and they are not bound by the "duty to co-operate" - a duty that applies to all other plan making bodies[3].

Once in place however, neighbourhood plans have just as much impact on the determination of planning decisions as any other development plan document. This is because they become part of the "development plan" and this document has an important role, recognised and enshrined in the law related to the determination of planning applications.

Planning Decisions – The Legal Test

Planning decision-making is one of the key regulatory functions carried out by public bodies in England. It can unlock or freeze the development potential – and financial value – of land and so has significant consequences both for the community and the land affected. The decision maker is most usually a local authority planning officer or committee, but the decision-making function may be taken on by a planning inspector or the Secretary of State for Communities and Local Government.

Whoever makes the decision is required to do so in a particular way and within the context of a specific legal test. The current version of the legal test is an awkward conflation of two separate pieces of legislation:

- Section 70(1) of the 1990 Act requires the local authority to 'have regard to the provisions of the development plan,

3 S33A Planning and Compulsory Purchase Act 2004

so far as material to the application, and to any other material considerations';

- Section 38(6) of the 2004 Act informs and modifies this by adding the additional requirement that: 'if regard is to be had to the development plan…the determination must be made in accordance with the plan unless material considerations indicate otherwise.'

The legal test has legislative origins but has always had the effect of yoking law and policy together in a complex interactive process. The decision maker must consider every individual application against a specific policy context comprising both the development plan policies relevant to the land and a wide range of relevant planning issues, where they are 'material' to the particular application. The decision maker has a broad range of potential choices: which development plan policies to choose; which considerations are more or less material than the others, and how they should be weighed against each other in deciding whether or not to grant permission. In this process of balancing and assessment the weight given to policies, their impact in relation to particular applications is not fixed but can instead fluctuate depending on the writer, the reader and the physical and political context within which they are read and understood.

The complexity of this balancing process, the extent to which it involves the exercise of relatively subjective judgments by local authorities and the significance in both financial and community terms of the decisions taken in terms of their economic and social consequences have conspired to make this an enduringly dynamic, complex and controversial area of planning law. There is a substantial body of case law on every element of the test including the definition of the development plan; the meaning of material considerations and the relative weight to be given to each in the determination of individual applications.

The focus and balance of this decision-making process can be fundamentally shifted through the introduction by government of overarching policy presumptions. These presumptions are highly significant for their impact on the legal test. They are required to be taken into account so that a lack of proper regard to them will invalidate the decision as a whole. They effectively require the decision-maker to adopt a particular bias in relation to the proposal even before the normal weighing process begins. When applied through government policy they leave the words of the legal test untouched but influence its application in a fundamental way, by requiring a particular orientation to be applied by the decision maker. Generally, they make the delicate task of juggling development plan policies against material considerations even more complex and potentially hazardous for the decision maker.

The current planning system operates with a presumption in favour of the development plan introduced as an amendment to the 1990 Act and confirmed in subsequent policy documents. In the landmark *City of Edinburgh* case in 1997 Lord Clyde ruled that that: "...the development plan is no longer simply one of the material considerations...there is now a presumption that the development plan is to govern the decision on an application for planning permission."[4] This judgment was reinforced by subsequent policy documents and the presumption still remains in place.

Development plans are therefore a primary consideration in the determination of planning applications. The decision maker must

---

4 City of Edinburgh Council v. Secretary of State for Scotland and Others [1997] UKHL 38 [11]

consider a wide and sometimes conflicting range of policy aims and ambitions and decide whether or not a particular application is 'in accordance with' that development plan. Plans are so broad in scope so that it is almost always possible to use their content to create and present legitimate arguments both in favour of, and against, the proposal at hand based. The difficulty of the exercise was recently summarised in the 2012 *Tesco Stores* case where Lord Reed commented that "development plans are full of broad statements of policy, many of which may be mutually irreconcilable". [5] Nevertheless, the decision maker is required to consider each application for its compliance with the plan 'as a whole', deciding which policies are relevant and taking into account the extent to which a particular proposal accords with them or not.

The process is neither simple nor static and may be made more complex where the 'development plan' comprises more than one document. Development proposals in London must also take into account the strategic ambitions of the London Plan as well as the plan for the individual Borough. And where an NDP has been made, it too must be taken into account.

Planning Decisions – Material Considerations

Having identified the development plan, the relevant development plan policies, and considered whether or not the current application is in accordance with them, the next task facing the decision maker is to identify the full range of other considerations material to that application, and then decide whether the initial decision-making inclination is either confirmed or confounded by them.

---

5 Tesco Stores Limited (Appellants) v Dundee City Council (Respondents) (Scotland) [2012] UKSC 13 [19]

The concept of material considerations has been in place as a key element of the legal test since 1947. The leading case is still *Stringer*[6] which established that any consideration relating to the use or development of land could be 'capable' of being a material consideration in the assessment of an application for planning permission, though whether it was or not would depend on the particular proposal and its circumstances. This broad range of potential material considerations was, if anything, widened with the 1995 *Tesco* decision that established that regard must be paid by the decision maker to any consideration with 'some connection with the proposed development which is not de minimis'.[7]

The understanding of what is or is not material can evolve over time and be modified so that considerations previously considered irrelevant become issues that ought to be taken into account. To this extent material considerations function as a social and political barometer reflecting both societal concerns and changes in political perspective. For example, public health concerns previously seen as irrelevant have, with concerns about obesity and public health, gained status as material planning considerations, so that in *Copeland* the grant of permission for a change of use from grocery shop to fast food takeaway was invalidated because the council did not consider the proximity of the takeaway to a local school as a material consideration[8].

Government policy, whether contained in the Framework, the online National Planning Policy Guidance, or and parliamentary white papers and ministerial statements, will always be material to a planning decision. Indeed the recent *Frack Free Balcombe* case

6 Stringer v Minister of Housing and Local Government [1971] 1 All E.R.65 [77]

7 Tesco Stores Ltd v Secretary of State for the Environment [1995] 1 WLR 759 [44]

8 R (Copeland) v London Borough of Tower Hamlets [2010] EWHC 1845 (Admin)

confirmed that "national Planning Policy is par excellence a material consideration." [9] Other issues that are routinely considered to be material considerations when relevant to any application include: alternative potential uses for the land; the planning history of the site; the potential for creating a precedent for similar developments in the area; the availability of alternative sites for the use; relevant appeal decisions; and parallel statutory codes such as licensing of premises health and safety, and building control.

The age and relevance of the development plan will always be a material consideration. As shown above, plan policies formulated under a different national or local context or an altered economic environment can quickly become out of date when the in the face of changing national policies such as the Framework. In such circumstances the principle established in *Simpson Corporation* applies; the local authority need not 'slavishly adhere' to the plan policies but may instead allow material considerations to weigh more heavily in the planning balance[10]. The local authority whose adopted plan is out of date and/or inconsistent with emerging national policies, or its own local plan, must recognise and take that age and inconsistency into account, and where necessary give increased weight to more up-to-date policies, whether emerging nationally or through the development and adoption of a replacement plan. Paragraph 216 of the Framework confirms the principle previously established in guidance and case law: the nearer an emerging policy is to adoption, and the fewer unresolved objections remain, the greater weight it will have in the decision-making process.

---

9 Frack Free Balcombe Residents Association, R (on the Application of) v West Sussex County Council [2014] EWHC 4108 (Admin)

10 Simpson v. Edinburgh Corporation, 1960 SC 313

Planning Decisions – The Planning Balance and the Tilted Balance

The exercise of balancing policies against material considerations is process is commonly, though not formally, referred to as "the planning balance". However, the cancellation, by the Coalition government of 2010 of Planning Policy Statement 1 and its replacement with the Framework introduced a new presumption and, with it, the notion of another widely used phrase – the 'tilted balance'.

On the one hand, the Framework explicitly restates and reinforces the status quo of the legal test. Paragraph 11 states that applications should be decided in accordance with the development plan unless material considerations indicate otherwise. Paragraphs 12, 32 and 50 reinforce this position so that the development plan is preserved as the 'starting point' for decision making with the Framework as no more than a new material consideration. On the other hand, paragraph 14 of the Framework introduces a new presumption in favour of sustainable development, described as a "golden thread running through both plan-making and decision-taking" paragraph 14 states that "For decision-taking this means:

- approving development proposals that accord with the development plan without delay; and

- where the development plan is absent, silent or relevant policies are out-of-date, granting permission unless: – any adverse impacts of doing so would significantly and demonstrably outweigh the benefits, when assessed against the policies in this Framework taken as a whole; or – spe-

> cific policies in this Framework indicate development should be restricted.

Sustainable Development itself has no formal definition in the Framework but paragraph 6 of the Framework states that "The policies in paragraphs 18 to 219, taken as a whole, constitute the Government's view of what sustainable development in England means in practice for the planning system".

The effect of these two paragraphs in terms of planning decisions is to create a requirement for the decision maker dealing with a plan that has "absent, silent or relevant policies" to apply a presumption in favour of sustainable development. In Bloor Homes Mr Justice Lindblom comprehensively explored and defined the circumstances in which the presumption might apply, ruling that:

- A development plan will be "absent" if none has been adopted for the relevant area;
- ...it may be "silent" because it lacks policy relevant to the project under consideration;
- ...relevant policies...may have been overtaken by things that have happened since it was adopted...

Labelling them as the 'three possible shortcomings' of a development plan, he was equally clear that any of them, if present, would impose a requirement, in the form of the presumption, that planning permission be granted[11]. When it applies, the new presumption operates in favour of all development proposals.

11 Bloor Homes East Midlands Ltd v Secretary of State for Communities and Local Government & Anor [2014] EWHC 754 (Admin)

The Neighbourhood Plan as Development Plan

Neighbourhood plans are therefore introduced into an established, and complex, decision-making process as one of a number of documents that comprise the adopted development plan. It is fair to say that they have had much more impact than anyone expected when they were first conceived – particularly where a neighbourhood plan is adopted, or close to adoption, while the host local authority has an out of date plan and has no prospect of quickly adopting a replacement. In such circumstances, the adopted neighbourhood plan may be the only development plan in place, so that its policies are extremely significant for development proposals in the area it covers.

The 2014 Report of the Communities and Local Government Committee on the operation of the Framework noted this potential conflict and the resulting confusion, recommending that the Government carry out an immediate consultation on it[12]. No such consultation has occurred. In the meantime, the NPPG is clear that "decision makers should include within their assessment those policies in the Framework that deal with neighbourhood planning. This includes paragraph 185:

- "185… Once a neighbourhood plan has demonstrated its general conformity with the strategic policies of the Local Plan and is brought into force, the policies it contains take precedence over existing non-strategic policies in the Local Plan for that neighbourhood, where they are in conflict. Local planning authorities should avoid duplicating planning processes for non-strategic policies where a neighbourhood plan is in preparation

12 Communities and Local Government Committee, *Operation of the National Planning Policy Framework* (HC 2014-15)

A number of cases have considered the scope and effect of the neighbourhood plan in this context but the judiciary has not so far limited the impact of NDP policies as a result:

- In *Gladman*[13] Mr Justice Lewis confirmed that a neighbourhood development plan may include policies dealing with the use and development of land for housing, including policies dealing with the location of a proposed number of new dwellings, even where there is at present no development plan document setting out strategic polices for housing adding that "there is nothing … to support the contention that a neighbourhood development plan cannot include policies dealing with the use and development of land for housing in the absence of a development plan document setting out strategic policies on housing issues.

- In *Woodcock Holdings*[14] Mr Justice Holgate ruled that "Although a neighbourhood plan must be in general conformity with the strategic policies of the local plan …these principles do not apply where a neighbourhood plan is progressed in advance of the adoption of any local plan. The absence of a local plan does not preclude the preparation and formal approval of a neighbourhood plan.

- In *Langmead*[15] Mrs Justice Lang considered the decision of a planning inspector to refuse permission for a devel-

13 Gladman Developments Ltd, R (on the application of) v Aylesbury Vale District Council & Ors [2014] EWHC 4323 (Admin) URL: http://www.bailii.org/ew/cases/EWHC/Admin/2014/4323.html

14 Woodcock Holdings Ltd v Secretary of State for Communities And Local Government & Anor [2015] EWHC 1173 (Admin) URL: http://www.bailii.org/ew/cases/EWHC/Admin/2015/1173.html

15 Keith Langmead Ltd v Secretary of State for Communities and Local Government & Anor [2017] EWHC 788 (Admin)

opment on grounds including conflict with the Yapton Neighbourhood Plan, and upheld his conclusion that the development proposal did not comply with "*the social element of sustainability*" because of its conflict with that plan.

In *DLA Delivery*[16] Lord Justice Lindblom confirmed that: “Housing allocations made in a neighbourhood development plan for a plan period which does not coincide or even overlap with the period of an adopted local plan cannot logically be said to lack "general conformity" in this respect.” In terms of its status as a development plan document, therefore, it is clear that NDPs can not only supplement the existing plans but may also set strategic policies, including those for the allocation of housing, even in the absence of an up to date local authority plan.

The 2017 Act also introduced changes confirming the status of the plan

- Section 1 of the 2017 Act, brought into force on 17th July 2017 by Regulation 2a of the Neighbourhood Planning Act 2017 (Commencement No 1) Regulations [17]require a local planning authority or other planning decision-taker to have regard to a post-examination neighbourhood development plan when dealing with an application for planning permission, so far as that plan is material to the application.

- Section 2 of the Neighbourhood Planning Act 2017, brought into force by Regulation 3 of the Town and

16 DLA Delivery Ltd, R (On the Application Of) v Lewes District Council [2017] EWCA Civ 58 . URL: http://www.bailii.org/ew/cases/EWCA/Civ/2017/58.html

17 SI2017/767

Country Planning, England Neighbourhood Planning Act 2017 (Commencement No 3) Regulations 2018[18] amends Schedule 1 to the 1990 Act to require a local planning authority, or the Secretary of State, to notify neighbourhood planning bodies of planning applications (or alterations to applications) in their area. This requirement applies when there is a neighbourhood development plan which forms part of the statutory development plan, or when there is a post-examination neighbourhood development plan (as defined by section 1 of the Act) in place, for a neighbourhood area all or part of which falls within the authority's area, unless the body has given notification in writing that it does not wish to be notified of any such application.

The Neighbourhood Plan as a Material Consideration

As with any other development plan, it is easy for an NDP to become out of date when, as is normal in planning, another 'superior' plan is adopted that contains conflicting policies. In such circumstances the NDP will not have the same significance as an adopted and up to date development plan. This has been confirmed in two cases.

- In *Gladman* [19] Mr Justice Lewis confirmed that in the event that the local planning authority subsequently makes a development plan document that does include strategic

18 SI 2018/38

19 Gladman Developments Ltd, R (on the application of) v Aylesbury Vale District Council & Ors [2014] EWHC 4323 (Admin) URL: *http://www.bailii.org/ew/cases/EWHC/Admin/2014/4323.html*

policies, that document will be part of the development plan and, as a later policy, will prevail over any inconsistent policies in the earlier neighbourhood development plan: see section 38(5) of the 2004 Act.

- More recently in *DLA Delivery*[20] Lord Justice Lindblom ruled that "If a neighbourhood development plan has been made and the local planning authority later produces a development plan document containing new "strategic policies", that development plan document will, under section 38(5) of the 2004 Act, prevail over any inconsistent policies in the neighbourhood development plan.

However, this does not mean that the NDP will not be considered at all. In the *DLA* case Lord Justice Lindblom went on to rule that "if a policy in a neighbourhood development plan is not, or ceases to be, up-to-date, this will be a material consideration in a development control decision and may justify departing from that policy. It is clear therefore that an emerging NDP, or an 'out of date' NDP will still be a significant element in the decision-making process, as a material consideration and in the same way as any other out of date development plan policy.

Summary

The legal test for the determination of planning applications is far more complex in nature than is apparent from the bare text of the relevant sections. The balancing process is unique to each proposal and is technically for the decision-maker alone. The development plan must be identified and taken into account as a primary con-

20 DLA Delivery Ltd, R (On the Application Of) v Lewes District Council [2017] EWCA Civ 58. URL: *http://www.bailii.org/ew/cases/EWCA/Civ/2017/58.html*

sideration, but it must also be weighed against the other considerations material to that decision. Material considerations are unique to each case and mutate according to circumstance, including through alterations to legislation or by new central government policy, or through ministerial statements. The weighing of the relative weight of development plan policies against material considerations is a concealed, complex, protean process that adapts to fit an ever-changing socio-political context and serve a variety of political ideologies, with politicians rather than planners or planning lawyers as the final arbiters in any such decision.

NDPs are new participants in this decision-making process and but the amount of case law generated alone shows the impact they have made since their introduction in 2011. There is no sign of this impact diminishing. Local authorities continue to struggle to make plans and keep them up to date in a rapidly changing policy context, while NDPs are relatively simple to make and certainly quicker and continue to enjoy cross-party political support supported by key legislative developments.

PART THREE

Introduction

So far this book has focussed on the general context surrounding, and role of the NDP in the English planning process; this and the following sections examine in much more detail how an NDP is made and adopted. The first two steps in that process – are the official recognition of the community body as a neighbourhood forum or "Qualifying Body" for the purposes of the legislation, and the designation of a particular piece of land – the "Neighbourhood Area" – that will be the covered by the NDP policies.

Designation – Qualifying Body

Section 38A of the 2004 Act and section 61E of the 1990 Act confer power on a Qualifying Body to make a plan and define that body as "a parish council, or an organisation or body designated as a neighbourhood forum"[1]. The application process is governed by section 61F (5) of the 1990 Act[2] and Regulations 8-12 of the 2012 regulations.

Section 61F (1) of the 1990 Act authorises a Parish Council to act as the qualifying body where the area of the proposed plan "consists of or includes the whole or any part of" the administrative area of the Parish Council. Where there is no existing Parish Council, the community needs to create its own dedicated organisation or group and then have it formally recognised.

1 Section 61E(6) of the 1990 Act

2 Although section 61F refers to neighbourhood development orders, its provisions are applied to NDPS by section 38C (2)(a) of the 2004 Act.

Section 61F (5) requires that the Forum must be established for the express purpose of promoting or improving the social, economic and environmental well-being of an area, must have a minimum of 21 members and with a membership open to individuals who live in the neighbourhood area concerned, or work there, or are elected members of the local county or district council or London Borough, and must have a written constitution. The question of what constitutes a community body has not been tested in the context of neighbourhood planning but there is some helpful judicial guidance in a case relating to Assets of Community Value – another relatively new area of law where community organisations are created for planning purposes. The First Tier Tribunal of the General Regulatory Chamber has considered the meaning of a community body in the context of an application to designate a pub as a community asset.[3] In that case Judge Peter Lane applied the normal dictionary meaning of body which is an "organised group of people with a common function". This included unincorporated associations but could apply more broadly; it was enough that a number of individuals came "together to further a matter of common interest".

Regulation 8 requires the application to include the name of the proposed neighbourhood forum; a copy of the written constitution of the proposed neighbourhood forum; the name of the neighbourhood area to which the application relates, a map which identifies the area, the contact details of at least one member of the proposed neighbourhood forum and a statement which explains how the proposed neighbourhood forum meets the requirements of section 61F(5).

---

3 Mendoza Ltd v London Borough Of Camden & Anor (Localism Act 2011) [2016] UKFTT CR-2015-0015 (GRC)
URL: http://www.bailii.org/uk/cases/UKFTT/GRC/2016/CR-2015-0015.html

Once submitted, the application process is regulated by section 61F(7) and Regulation 9. Section 61F(7) requires the local authority to have regard to the desirability of designation, taking into account compliance with regulation 5, the diversity of the membership and the extent to which the purpose of the body reflects the character of the area. Regulation 9 requires the local authority to publicise the application on their website and "in such other manner as they consider is likely to bring the application to the attention of people who live, work or carry on business in the area to which the application relates" including a copy of the application; a statement that if a designation is made no other organisation or body may be designated for that neighbourhood area until that designation expires or is withdrawn; details of how to make representations; and the date by which those representations must be received - allowing at least 6 weeks for this.

The Housing and Planning Act 2016 included provisions to speed up and simplify the NDP process including enabling the Secretary of State to prescribe dates for compliance with certain requirements including designation of the qualifying body. Regulations made under this Section 139 of the 2016 Act[4] inserted a new regulation 9A to the 2012 Regulations so that local authorities are now required to determine the application:

- Within 20 weeks of the date on which the application is first publicised in a case where the neighbourhood area to which the application relates falls within the areas of two or more local planning authorities;

- Within 13 weeks of the date on which the application is first publicised in all other cases.

4 SI 2016/648

Once the decision is made, regulation 10 requires publication of the decision. If the decision is to designate, it must include the name of the neighbourhood forum; a copy of the written constitution of the neighbourhood forum; the name of the neighbourhood area to which the designation relates; and contact details for at least one member of the neighbourhood forum. Where is a decision is made not to designate, a statement must be published setting out the decision and their reasons for making the decision.

Regulation 11 allows subsequent applications to be refused where a neighbourhood forum has already been designated and Regulation 12 allows an application to be made for designation to be withdrawn. Designation ceases to have effect after 5 years, or if a new parish council is created in relation to the same area, or if it no longer complies with the conditions or other criteria taken into account at designation.

Designation – Relevant Area

Designation of an Area for the purpose of a Neighbourhood Plan is governed by Section 61G of the 1990 Act and Regulations 5-7 of the 2012 Regulations. The process of designation begins with an application being made by a Parish Council or neighbourhood forum. The area must be within the administrative area of that parish council or within the area specified by the neighbourhood forum in its application for designation, and there must not be any overlap with other areas designated.

Regulation 5 requires an application for designation of an area to include a map which identifies the area to which the area application relates; a statement explaining why this area is considered appropriate to be designated as a neighbourhood area; and a statement that the organisation or body making the area application is a relevant body for the purposes of section 61G of the 1990 Act. Regulation 6 requires an application to be publicised by the local authority, such publication to include a copy of the application, details of how to make representations; and the date by which those representations must be received.

Regulation 5A, introduced as a result of changes made by the Housing and Planning Act 2016, imposes an absolute requirement to designate an area where it mirrors that of an existing parish council area. When considering whether or not to approve an application for designation section 61G requires that the authority must have regard to the desirability of designating the whole of the area of a parish council as a neighbourhood area, and the desirability of maintaining the existing boundaries of areas already designated as neighbourhood areas but has a discretion to approve areas outside existing parish boundaries.

Regulation 6A of the 2012 Regulations requires an application for designation of an area to be determined within 13 weeks from first publication unless the application covers more than one local authority in which case a 20 week time limit applies. Regulation 7 requires that the decision must be publicised "as soon as possible" after it is made including:

- The date of designation;
- The name of the neighbourhood area;
- A map which identifies the area; and

- The name of the relevant body who applied for the designation.

If the applications is refused Regulation 7 also requires publication of the decision and a statement of their reasons for making that decision and details of where and when the decision document may be inspected.

The scope of the power to designate an area has been tested in the *Daws Hill* case where the Daws Hill Neighbourhood Forum challenged the decision of Wycombe District Council to designate a smaller area than applied for, specifically excluding two 'strategic' sites identified for development in the adopted Core Strategy. Mr Justice Supperstone ruled [5] that the section gave the planning authority a broad discretion, to be exercised with regard to the particular circumstances of the application. In this case, he recognised that by the time the plan was adopted development would be underway on those sites and the plan could not realistically influence that, and the challenge was not successful.

On appeal [6] the Forum raised the specific question of whether the discretion to decide on an appropriate area was to decide *whether* a given area should or should not be designated as a neighbourhood area, or was confined to a very narrow discretion to decide *within which* neighbourhood area any given site was to be included. The Court ruled that the discretion was not limited in the way that was proposed, but rather that the local authority was entitled to have regard to a wide range of planning considerations. Specifically it was within the scope of section 61G to designate an area smaller than that applied for.

---

5 http://www.bailii.org/ew/cases/EWHC/Admin/2013/513.html

6 R (Daws Hill Neighbourhood Forum) v. Wycombe District Council [2014] EWCA Civ 228; (6th March 2014)

Regulation 3(c) of the Neighbourhood Planning Act 2017 (Commencement No. 3) Regulations 2018 brings into force section 5 of the Neighbourhood Planning Act 2017. Section 5 amends the Town and Country Planning Act 1990 and the Planning and Compulsory Purchase Act 2004 to facilitate the modification of a neighbourhood area It includes provisions for designations to cease having effect if a new parish council is created, and the power to change the boundary of an existing neighbourhood area, to replace an existing neighbourhood area with two or more separate neighbourhood areas, to replace two or more existing neighbourhood areas with a single neighbourhood area, to split or combine neighbourhood areas. The commentary to the 2017 Act anticipates that these powers might be used "where a community governance review leads to changes to a parish boundary or the creation of a new parish, or where parish councils choose to undertake neighbourhood planning together or to plan for their own area where they have previously acted together."

Writing the Plan

Once there is a qualifying body and a designated area, the next task is to draft the plan itself. This is certainly the longest, and arguably the most demanding, part of the process and involves extensive and sustained collaboration between the members of the forum, the local community and the local planning authority. The content of the plan policies therefore will – and should – be generated by the local community – and as much as possible of the text of the policies should be the words of that community.

A lawyer can help to ensure that the presentation of policies is achieved in a way that will make them most palatable to the local authority and the examiner including the following:

- Division of the plan in to relevant chapters;

- Adopting a common structure for each policy ideally beginning with the text of the policy itself before supporting the policy with relevant subsections such as "explanation", "justification" etc;

- Critical consideration and inclusion of the evidence base for any assertions made or requirements imposed;

- Maintaining a glossary of terms including cross references to those already defined in other documents.

In terms of legislation, sections 38A -38B to the 2004 Act and section 61K of the Town and Country Planning Act 1990 are relevant:

- Section 38A defines a 'neighbourhood development plan' as 'a plan which sets out policies (however expressed) in relation to the development and use of land in the whole or any part of a particular neighbourhood area specified in the plan.'

- Section 38B deals with the form and contents of neighbourhood development plans. It requires that: 1) the plan must specify the period for which it is to have effect; 2) the plan may not include provision about development that is excluded development; 3) may not relate to more than one neighbourhood area.

- Section 61K defines "Excluded" development to include:

    - Development that consists of a "county matter" – this is development defined in Schedule 1 paragraph 1(1)(a) to (h) of the 1990 Act, broadly: mining and minerals development, quarrying activities and associated buildings and uses.

    - Development that consists of the carrying out of any operation, or class of operation, prescribed under paragraph 1(j) of the same Schedule – this is waste development.

    - Development that falls within Annex 1 to Council Directive 85/337/EEC on the assessment of the effects of certain public and private projects on the environment – this is major infrastructure works recognised as having significant effects on the environment including long-distance railway lines, motorways and express roads, airports, and major installations for the disposal of hazardous and non-hazardous waste, and waste water treatment plants.

    - Development that consists (whether wholly or partly) of a nationally significant infrastructure project. These are defined by section 14 of the Planning Act 2008 and include generating stations, underground gas storage and pipelines, airports, harbours, railways, damns, hazardous waste and waste water treatment plants.

- o Prescribed development or development of a prescribed description.

- o Development in a prescribed area or an area of a prescribed description.

The courts considered the meaning of 'excluded development' in the 2017 *Hoare* case[7], a challenge to the decision of the Vale of White Horse District Council to accept the Faringdon Neighbourhood Plan and proceed to a referendum on it. One of the policies provided that a local quarry should be safeguarded for employment uses, subject to satisfying specified criteria. Part of the basis for the challenge was that this policy related to "excluded development", and that its inclusion invalidated the plan as a whole. Mr Justice Howell was very clear that the argument was "untenable…there is nothing to preclude a neighbourhood development plan making provision about a development that may be carried out on land subject to such conditions…There is equally no bar on a neighbourhood plan containing policies for development that may have significant effects on the environment."

In terms of securing advice on writing the plan itself, some local authorities have produced their own and where they have it makes sense to have any such guidelines in mind and observe them as much as possible. For more general advice, other possible starting points include:

- Locality[8] – the national membership network for community organisations. "We support community organisations to be strong and successful, to meet local

7 Hoare v The Vale of White Horse District & Ors [2017] EWHC 1711 (Admin)

8 https://locality.org.uk/about/

needs and to give people a purpose, a good place to live and good health."

- The Government's own pages of advice on neighbourhood planning[9]
- The Forum for Neighbourhood Planning[10]

Regulation 14 Engagement and Consultation

Once the plan has coalesced into a set of policies that are generally agreed to represent the aims and aspirations of that community in terms of consciously shaping their area, the qualifying body will start considering when the document should be formally submitted. Before any such submission occurs, a formal engagement/consultation exercise must be carried out as required by Regulation 14 of the 2012 Regulations.

Regulation 14 requires that the qualifying body must, prior to submission of a proposed plan to the relevant local authority:

- publicise, in a manner that is likely to bring it to the attention of people who live, work or carry on business in the neighbourhood area
    - details of the proposals for a neighbourhood development plan;

9 https://www.gov.uk/guidance/neighbourhood-planning--2

10 https://www.ourneighbourhoodplanning.org.uk/

  - o details of where and when the proposals for a neighbourhood development plan may be inspected;

  - o details of how to make representations;

  - o the date by which those representations must be received, being not less than 6 weeks from the date on which the draft proposal is first publicised;

- consult any consultation body referred to in paragraph 1 of Schedule 1 whose interests the qualifying body considers may be affected by the proposals for a neighbourhood development plan; and

- send a copy of the proposals for a neighbourhood development plan to the local planning authority.

At first sight, the list of consultation bodies in Schedule 1 is daunting; the Schedule lists an enormous number of consultees – including the Coal Authority, and the Marine Management Organisation. However it is important to remember that the regulation itself states that they should only be consulted where the qualifying body considers that their interests "may be affected by the proposals", which will reduce the list considerably in most circumstances.

Even though there is no need to contact each and every organisation in Schedule 1 it is good practice for the qualifying body to go through the list and note formally which will and will not be consulted and why. The local authority should be advised of the choices made and given an opportunity to comment on it to avoid problems later in the process.

Where the plan is making a strong case for allocation of infrastructure, it is a good idea in any case to consult organisations such as the clinical commissioning groups to ensure that the plan takes into account the actual infrastructure needs as identified by the relevant infrastructure providers. Schedule 1 also lists as potential consultees "voluntary bodies some or all of whose activities benefit all or any part of the neighbourhood area", and bodies that represent the interests of 1) different racial, ethnic or national;2) different religious groups in the neighbourhood area; 3) persons carrying on business in the neighbourhood area; and d) bodies which represent the interests of disabled persons in the neighbourhood area. Again, it is good practice to include all such organisations as a matter of course because if one or more of them is missed out it may make it difficult to show that there was compliance with the Public Sector Equality Duty.

Consultation – Common Law Principles and Guidance

Consultation is an important element of many of the stages in making a neighbourhood plan. For some elements of the plan process the 2012 Regulations are very clear on what is required, however others impose a very general consultation requirement to publicise decisions or documents "on their website and in such other manner as they consider is likely to bring the application to the attention of people who live, work or carry on business in the area to which the application relates"

In all of these circumstances, while there is a clear need to consult and be seen to do so properly, it is much less clear what is required in order for the legal requirements to be met. This leaves room for interpretation – and for challenges based on an alternative interpretation of the formal requirements – resulting in a need for the qualifying body to develop some awareness of the relevant procedural context.

The primary source of common law principles relating to consultation are the *Gunning Principles* that can be summarised as follows:

- Consultation must take place when the proposal is still at a formative stage: This principle does not mean that the decision-maker has to consult on all possible options of achieving a particular objective, but it does require a transparently open mindset to be adopted from the start.

- Sufficient reasons must be put forward for the proposal to allow for intelligent consideration and response: Consultees should be made aware of the basis on which a proposal for consultation has been considered and will thereafter be considered. Those consulted should be aware of the criteria that will be applied when considering proposals and what factors will be considered 'decisive' or 'of substantial importance' at the end of the process.

- Adequate time must be given for consideration and response: Unless statutory time requirements are prescribed, there is no necessary time frame within which the consultation must take place. The decision-maker may adopt a policy as to the necessary time-frame (e.g. Cabinet Office guidance, or compact with the voluntary sector), and if it wishes to depart from that policy it should have a good reason for doing so. Otherwise, it may be guilty of a breach of a legitimate expectation that the policy will be adhered to.

- The product of consultation must be conscientiously taken into account: If the decision-maker does not properly consider the material produced by the consultation, then it can be accused of having made up its mind; or of failing to take into account a relevant consideration.

There are also some useful external sources of guidance. The Cabinet Office has its own consultation guidance, which should be read and applied where practical[11] and it will certainly be worth looking at the local authority's own Statement of Community Involvement – or "SCI" as this will set out the local authority's standards and practice in terms of community engagement and consultation that should be followed as closely as possible.

Ideally the scope of publicity for the plan should be as wide and imaginative as possible involving community bodies, business associations, and social media forums as well as the more standard methods such as letter drops and formal consultations. However, there is some risk in relying on electronic consultation alone, as is demonstrated by *Kendall v Rochford District Council.*[12] One of the key issues was the validity of electronic consultation for complying with statutory requirements in the case of a draft development plan document. The judge commented that sole reliance on a website consultation "was not an effective means of consulting the public" and that "members of the public … would not have been aware that consultation under the SEA regulations was taking place unless they happened to have heard about it by chance."

---

11 https://www.gov.uk/government/publications/consultation-principles-guidance

12 Kendall v Rochford District Council & Ano [2014] EWHC 3866 (Admin) http://www.bailii.org/ew/cases/EWHC/Admin/2014/3866.html

PART FOUR

Regulation 15 Submission

This is one of the most significant parts of the whole process. For the qualifying body, it is the point where everything they have done to that point will be evaluated and scrutinised against a wide and relatively complex set of procedural requirements. For the local authority, it is the point where management of the process and compliance with the legal requirements falls primarily within its responsibility. It is also the point where the plan becomes visible to the public as a whole including, potentially, organisations and individuals who may not agree with the plan and could be seeking to delay or prevent its adoption.

The qualifying body must consider the requirements of Paragraph 1 of Schedule 4B of the 1990 act and Regulation 15 itself. Paragraph 1 of the Schedule requires the proposal to include a draft of the Plan, a statement summarising its contents and why it should be made, copies to be sent to 'persons prescribed" and to be compliant generally with regulations or guidance published by the Secretary of State. Regulation 15 requires that the following documents need to be submitted:

- A map or statement identifying the area which the proposed neighbourhood development plan relates to.

- The consultation statement.

- An environmental report or a formal statement as to why this is not required.

- A statement explaining how the basic conditions have been complied with.

Consultation Statement

The need for engagement – and the common law principles that operate in relation to it – are examined above. Apart from being a fundamental element of good practice in any plan process, consultation is also formally required by Regulation 15 which requires that submission of the draft plan – is accompanied by a 'consultation statement'. This is defined in Regulation 15 as "a document which:

- contains details of the persons and bodies who were consulted about the proposed neighbourhood development plan;
- explains how they were consulted;
- summarises the main issues and concerns raised by the persons consulted; and
- describes how these issues and concerns have been considered and, where relevant, addressed in the proposed neighbourhood development plan.

At some point, whatever the content and outcome of any informal engagement and consultation, that process will need to be summarised in the form of a document that complies with this regulation. In order to make the process as painless as possible, it is recommended that the designated body keeps a good record of who was consulted or engaged with, when that consultation or engagement was carried out, a note of the response – or lack of response – in each case, and whether any changes were made to the plan as a result. It is also good practice to start a draft of the consultation statement before any engagement exercise is undertaken, and to ensure that it is regularly updated so that it evolves organically over the engagement process. It is even better practice to keep a post- submission record of any engagement activities, even after the date for submission of the statement is passed as it will be a really useful source of information for the examiner as well as potentially valuable in any future proceedings.

Environmental Report

The Environmental Report is a key element of the Regulation 15 submission. It is one part of the neighbourhood plan process that is regulated by European requirements so the environmental report is also a fundamental part of compliance with "EU Obligations" considered below. The Strategic Environmental Assessment Protocol was adopted by an Extraordinary meeting of the Parties to the Espoo Convention, held on 21 May 2003 and ratified by the EU on 21 November 2008. The SEA Directive transposes the Protocol into EU legislation[1] and implemented into UK legislation by the Environmental Assessment of Plans and Programmes Regulations 2004.[2]

The aim of the SEA Directive is "to ensure that an environmental assessment is carried out of certain plans and programmes which are likely to have significant effects on the environment." The SEA Directive requires that the environmental effect of any plan or pro-

1 Directive 2001/42/EC

2 S.I. 2004 No. 1633

gramme which sets the framework for future development consent must be assessed by the local authority – this is often referred to as the screening process. Where the effect is likely to be significant an environmental report must be prepared so that the effects can be fully assessed and, where possible, mitigated prior to adoption of the plan.

The effect is that for all 'plans or programmes' falling within the scope of the SEA Directive one of the following must be included:

- an environmental statement that identifies the negative – and positive – impacts of the plan in environmental terms and how they may be mitigated; or

- a decision from the local authority – commonly referred to as a "screening" assessment" that the plan does not require an environmental statement to be supplied.

Neighbourhood plans fall within the scope of the SEA Directive. Some neighbourhood plans do need a full assessment, some do not, but all must be assessed for their potential impacts and in all cases a decision whether or not to require an environmental report must be made and recorded by the local authority. The impact of the provisions in relation to NDPs were clarified in 2015 with the Neighbourhood Planning (General) (Amendment) Regulations 2015[3] which amended regulation 15 of the 2012 regulations to include a general requirement to submit:

- an environmental report prepared in accordance with paragraphs (2) and (3) of regulation 12 of the Environmental Assessment of Plans and Programmes Regulations 2004; or

3 S.I. 2015/20

- where it has been determined under regulation 9(1) of those Regulations that the plan proposal is unlikely to have significant environmental effects (and, accordingly, does not require an environmental assessment), a statement of reasons for the determination].

In practice this means that the qualifying body must submit a report to the local authority, the content of which will be guided by the 2004 Regulations require to:

- Identify, describe and evaluate the likely significant effects on the environment of—implementing the plan or programme; and reasonable alternatives taking into account the objectives and the geographical scope of the plan or programme.

- Include other information "as may reasonably be required" taking into account current knowledge and methods of assessment; the contents and level of detail in the plan or programme; the stage of the plan or programme in the decision-making process; and the extent to which certain matters are more appropriately assessed at different levels in that process in order to avoid duplication of the assessment.

The local authority will then carry out a "screening assessment" of the plan. If that assessment considers that the plan is likely to have a significant impact then the relevant body must carry out a full appraisal of the likely impacts, along with any reasonable alternatives.

The requirement for submission of an environmental report and its assessment by the local authority has been considered a number of times by the courts. In one case lack of compliance resulted in the NDP being quashed so this is not an issue that can be ignored.

- In the *Gladman*[4] case, Mr Justice Lewis confirmed that the Council had prepared an assessment that was compliant with the statutory requirements, including identifying alternatives, and that the examiner had correctly concluded that compliance had been achieved.

- In *Larkfleet Homes*[5] the decision in question was the local authority conclusion that an NDP was not likely to have significant environmental effects and that an SEA was therefore not required in respect of it. The Court of Appeal decision was a useful reminder that positive as well as negative impacts had to be considered – and that if they were not the decision would be invalid – but ruled that in these particular circumstances it was "improbable in the extreme that anyone considering the SEAs for the Council's documents would have failed to appreciate that they examined positive as well as negative effects" and the challenge was unsuccessful.

- *DLA Delivery*[6] also questioned a local authority's conclusion – in this case that an assessment of the Habitats Directive was not required – but was also unsuccessful as

4 Gladman Developments Ltd, R (on the application of) v Aylesbury Vale District Council & Ors [2014] EWHC 4323 (Admin) URL: *http://www.bailii.org/ew/cases/EWHC/Admin/2014/4323.html*

5 Larkfleet Homes Ltd, R (on the application of) v Rutland County Council & Ors [2015] EWCA Civ 597 (17 June 2015) URL: *http://www.bailii.org/ew/cases/EWCA/Civ/2015/597.html*

6 DLA Delivery Ltd, R (On the Application Of) v Lewes District Council [2017] EWCA Civ 58 (10 February 2017) URL: *http://www.bailii.org/ew/cases/EWCA/Civ/2017/58.html*

Lord Justice Lindblom ruled that the decision was reasonable, even on the basis of very little evidence. He went on to comment that "Lord Justice Lindblom disagreed and confirmed that the court must avoid an overly stringent approach to a "screening" decision under regulations 5 and 9 of the SEA regulations – as this was "essentially a planning judgment".

- In *BDW Trading Ltd*[7] the question was raised as to whether the sustainability assessment was sufficient to meet the requirements of the SEA Directive. Mr Justice Supperstone stressed that the assessment needed only to include information "reasonably required" and could reasonably take into account the content and level of detail of the plan and its stage in the decision-making process.

Stonegate Homes[8] remains the only successful challenge to an NDP on the basis of non-compliance with the SEA Directive. The independent examiner concluded that "the SA/SEA demonstrates the revised NDPs policies will have no significant social, economic or environmental effect" but this was based largely on an assertion that this was "what the community felt". Mrs Justice Lang was clear that this was insufficient: "The obligation under the SEA Directive is to ensure that the consideration of reasonable alternatives is based upon an accurate picture of what reasonable alternatives are. That was not done here. Not only was the conclusion wrong but, in the circumstances, it was irrational, given the absence of an evidence base." In particular she commented

7 BDW Trading Ltd (t/a Barratt Homes) & Anor v Cheshire West & Chester Borough Council & Ors [2014] EWHC 1470 (Admin) URL: *http://www.bailii.org/ew/cases/EWHC/Admin/2014/1470.html*

8 Stonegate Homes Ltd & Anor, R (On the Application Of) v Horsham District Council [2016] EWHC 2512 (Admin) (13 October 2016) *http://www.bailii.org/ew/cases/EWHC/Admin/2016/2512.html*

that "The planning workshop did not provide a basis for supporting a contention that sites on the west would lead to unsustainable pressure on the local road network." The decision to make the plan was quashed.

Local Authority Consideration of Plan

The local authority will receive the documents submitted and given them consideration. If they are minded to accept the plan must consider all of the following issues[9]:

- Whether the qualifying body is authorised to act in relation to the neighbourhood area concerned.
- Whether the qualifying body has complied with the requirements in section 61 generally.
- Whether the proposal and the documents and information accompanying it (including the draft neighbourhood development order) complies with paragraph 1 of the Schedule.
- Whether the body has complied with the requirements of the regulations generally.

They should double check compliance with all of the matters referred to above and are likely to make a formal decision, usually at Cabinet level, to accept the plan or not.

If the plan is accepted, the qualifying body will be notified and the local authority will move on to formal publication of the plan

9 Contained in Paragraph 6 of Schedule B of the 1990 Act

under Regulation 16. This requires the following details to be publicised "on their website and in such other manner as they consider is likely to bring the proposal to the attention of people who live, work or carry on business in the neighbourhood area":

- details of the plan proposal;
- details of where and when the plan proposal may be inspected;
- details of how to make representations;
- a statement that any representations may include a request to be notified of the local planning authority's decision under regulation 19 (the future decision whether or not to make the plan itself); and
- the date by which those representations must be received, being not less than 6 weeks from the date on which the plan proposal is first publicised.

The local authority is also required to notify any consultation body which is referred to in the consultation statement that the plan proposal has been received.

Paragraph 5 of Schedule 4B to the 1990 Act gives the local authority a limited right to refuse to consider the proposed plan if they consider that it is a "repeat proposal". This only applies if in the previous 2 years they have refused a plan that is "the same or similar" or a referendum has been held and less than half of the people voting voted in favour AND there has been no change in "relevant considerations" since. "Relevant considerations" are changes to relevant national policies, and guidance and strategic policies in the development plan for that area. If it does refuse the plan, the local authority has to notify the qualifying body of the decision and give reasons.

Selection of Examiner

If the local planning authority considers that Schedule 4B has been complied with, it must also move on to selection of an examiner, if it has not already begun the process. The formal requirements are set out in clause 7 of Schedule 4B, and they require that the person selected be independent of both authorities, not have any interest in the land affected and have appropriate qualifications and experience. The authority may only appoint a person to carry out the examination if the qualifying body consents and there is a default power under Clause 7(5) 5 for the Secretary of State to make the appointment. In addition there is a service, the Neighbourhood Planning Independent Examiner Referral Service or 'NPIERS', run by RICS that enables communities and local authorities to make applications to NPIERS free of charge to obtain an Independent Examiner from a panel of highly competent professionals.

The *Legard*[10] case included a claim that the neighbourhood forum representative played an "uncontrolled and pivotal role" in elements of the process including the choice of the Examiner. The person challenging the adoption of the plan claimed, among other grounds, that the process surrounding the selection of the Examiner was 'outwith' the provisions of the legislation and used this as part of its wider claim that the local authority acted in a biased manner. As a result, the question of how an examiner

10 Legard, R (On the Application Of) v The Royal Borough of Kensington and Chelsea [2018] EWHC 32 (Admin)

should be selected was considered in some detail. Mr Justice Dove included in the sources relied on for his judgment the NPIERS guidance on the appointment of an examiner. He referred to, and endorsed, the following recommendations contained in the guidance:

- The process of selecting an examiner should begin as soon as the Regulation 14 process was complete.
- The brief to the examiner should include "expected outputs".
- The qualifying body should be involved both in the completion of the application form for appointment of the examiner as well as the actual selection of the examiner.

The judge went on to recognise that it was "part and parcel" of the officer role to have a 'listening ear' and to take account of "legitimately expressed interests raised with them by the members of the public who they are employed to serve". He stated that it was "beyond argument" that the representative of the neighbourhood planning body had a "role to play" in the selection of the examiner. He concluded that "there was nothing untoward about the selection process", that "ultimately the well informed and fair-minded observer would not detect any element of apparent bias in the process" and that paragraph 7(4) of Schedule 4B was correctly observed. He went on to comment that it was "good sense in engaging the qualifying body, as occurred here, in the Examiner selection process so as to ensure that they consent to the individual who emerges from the selection process".

Once the examiner has been selected and the consultation period has finished the local authority must send to the examiner:

- The plan.
- The documents submitted in compliance with Regulation 15.
- Any information related to compliance with the Habitats Regulations (if required).
- Representations received in response to the publicising of the proposed plan.

From this point, the formal examination process begins, and will be led by the examiner – though it is likely that the local authority will want to have oversight of the process because any later challenge will be to the local authority, and not the examiner.

Examination

Paragraphs 7 to 11 of Schedule 4B set out the arrangements for the independent examination of proposed orders and plans. Although similar in nature to a local plan examination, they are not the same and very little detail is prescribed, in contrast with the detailed regulatory requirements that attach to the examination of local plans. For example, while setting up and administration of a local plan inquiry is subject to detailed regulations, in the case of a neighbourhood plan examination the local authority must simply make “such arrangements as they consider appropriate”.

The NPIERS recommendations are therefore particularly useful in this context and should be borne in mind and complied with in as much detail as possible including the following:

- There should be one point of contact when discussing process, to act as a focal point for all communications between the Examiner, the local authority, the qualifying body and third parties. It is a good idea for all parties to know, and agree, on who this will be.

- Documentation demonstrating that all procedural steps have been undertaken should be made available from the beginning of the process.

- If an appointed Examiner, LPA and QB meet before the examination begins, they should only discuss administrative arrangements including contracting and invoicing, and the logistics of the examination.

- The Council's role at the hearing (if there is one) should be discussed and agreed in advance with the qualifying body and the Examiner.

Although not formally required, it is good practice to ensure that all meetings are minuted, all arrangements are recorded in writing, and that all those records are made available to the public.

The examination is generally carried out by the examiner as "consideration of written representations" but the examiner may convene a hearing to hear oral representations about a particular issue at the hearing to ensure "adequate examination" of that issue or to give someone "a fair chance to put a case" (Sch 4B clause 9). It is for the examiner to decide how the hearing is conducted, but it must be in public – this means that all oral hearings will be public and all written submissions will be available to all participants. Where there is a hearing, questions are generally asked only by the examiner unless cross questioning is considered necessary.

The role of the examination and the subsequent consideration of the plan and the examiner's report by the local planning authority is a narrow one. In addressing the draft plan the examiner must consider:

- whether the draft neighbourhood plan meets the basic conditions (considered below);
- whether the draft neighbourhood plan complies with ss 38A and 38B of the Planning and Compulsory Purchase Act 2004 or any provision made thereunder (in practice this means the 2012 Regulations;
- whether the area for any referendum should be extended beyond the neighbourhood area to which the draft order relates; and
- such other matters as may be prescribed (none have been at the date of writing this book).[11]

---

11 Town and Country Planning Act 1990, Sch 4B, para 8(1).

PART FIVE

Basic Conditions – Summary

A traditional local plan must comply with a range of legal requirements including the Duty to Cooperate with other public bodies, be shown to be "sound" which itself involves four further standards: positively prepared, justified, effective and consistent with national policy, and identify a five year supply of specific deliverable sites that should be updated annually.

In contrast a Neighbourhood plan requires compliance with the 'Basic Conditions" contained in paragraph 8(2) of Schedule B to the 1990 Act.[1] Compliance with these conditions is a fundamental requirement in determining whether an NDP is valid. Although the first time they are formally considered is by the Examiner during the examination process, their existence, and compliance with them, should be a primary concern both for the qualifying body and the relevant local authority throughout the plan process. Paragraph 8(2) states that a draft order meets the basic conditions if:

(a) having regard to national policies and advice contained in guidance issued by the Secretary of State, it is appropriate to make the order,

(b) having special regard to the desirability of preserving any listed building or its setting or any features of special architectural or historic interest that it possesses, it is appropriate to make the order,

1 Town and Country Planning Act 1990, Sch 4B, para 8(2)

(c) having special regard to the desirability of preserving or enhancing the character or appearance of any conservation area, it is appropriate to make the order,

(d) the making of the order contributes to the achievement of sustainable development,

(e) the making of the order is in general conformity with the strategic policies contained in the development plan for the area of the authority (or any part of that area),

(f) the making of the order does not breach, and is otherwise compatible with, EU obligations, and

(g) prescribed conditions are met in relation to the order and prescribed matters have been complied with in connection with the proposal for the order.

One of the most useful things a legal adviser can do while a plan is being drafted is to ensure that the content of the plan, and the plan-making process, continues to meet the requirements of the 'basic conditions". The details of that scrutiny will depend on the particular plan in consideration but as a minimum it is useful to ensure:

- that there is an ongoing awareness of relevant national and local policies and awareness of any emerging conflicts with them;
- that a robust definition of sustainable development is adopted and used as a basis for evaluation of policies;

- that listed buildings and conservation areas are specifically considered where relevant;
- that the 'EU obligations' examined in detail in the previous chapter are being complied with.

Conditions (a) (b) and (c) have not been considered by the courts, compliance with condition (g) relies on compliance with Section 61, and the 2012 Regulations rather than setting its own criteria. Conditions (d), (e) and (f) have been the subject of a number of cases, and these are worth examining in detail.

Condition d): Sustainable Development

Although there is no agreed or consistent definition of 'sustainable development' for neighbourhood plan purposes its meaning in the context of the NDP process is informed primarily by the treatment of that term in the Framework. The Framework "defines" sustainable development in three ways:

- The fundamental 'Brundtland' definition that proposes sustainable development as development that meets the needs of the present without compromising the needs of the future;
- The three 'dimensions' of sustainable development identified in the Framework: environmental, social and economic;
- The statement in paragraph 6 of the Framework which state that "The purpose of the planning system is to con-

> tribute to the achievement of sustainable development. The policies in paragraphs 18 to 219, taken as a whole, constitute the Government's view of what sustainable development in England means in practice for the planning system".

The term was formally considered in the 2014 case of *Gladman v Aylesbury Vale*[2]. Gladman Developments had earmarked three potential development sites in Winslow but they were not allocated for that purpose in Winslow Neighbourhood Plan. Gladman challenged the validity of the plan on a number of grounds and although non-compliance with Condition d) was not a specific ground of challenge, Mr Justice Lewis did consider this issue in his ruling. He confirmed that where an NDP was emerging in the absence of an up to date local authority plan, the examiner could legitimately conclude that condition 8(2)(d) has been satisfied, even if a future plan could require further development.

Condition e): General Conformity

Compliance with this condition has been challenged on a number of occasions. So far, none of the challenges have proved successful but the issue is nevertheless worth considering in detail.

---

2 Gladman Developments Ltd, R (on the application of) v Aylesbury Vale District Council & Ors [2014] EWHC 4323 (Admin) para 58, 60 URL: *http://www.bailii.org/ew/cases/EWHC/Admin/2014/4323.html*

The issue was considered in *BDW Trading v Cheshire West*[3] Mr Justice Supperstone ruled that the only statutory requirement imposed by Condition (e) was that the Neighbourhood Plan as a whole should be in general conformity with the adopted Development Plan as a whole. This position was supported in *Crownhall Estates*[4] where Mr Justice Holgate ruled that "Where it is engaged, the basic condition in paragraph 8(2)(e) of schedule 4B to TCPA 1990 only requires that the draft neighbourhood plan *as a whole* be in "general conformity" with the strategic policies of the adopted development plan (in so far as it exists) *as a whole*. Thus, there is no need to consider whether there is a conflict or tension between one policy of a neighbourhood plan and one element of the local plan" This position was supported by Mr Justice Kerr in *Kebbell Developments*[5] where he recognised that there was some tension between the emerging NDP and the relevant Local Plan but this was not enough to create a finding of general nonconformity.

The issue of conformity has been most contested, and most frequently argued, where a Neighbourhood Plan is being developed but the adopted local plan is out of date and inconsistent with national policies and the emerging plan is still at a very early stage. The argument has frequently been made that an examiner could not conclude that an NDP was in general conformity with rel-

---

3 BDW Trading Ltd (t/a Barratt Homes) & Anor v Cheshire West & Chester Borough Council & Ors [2014] EWHC 1470 (Admin) URL: http://www.bailii.org/ew/cases/EWHC/Admin/2014/1470.html para 82

4 Crownhall Estates Ltd, R (on the application of) v Chichester District Council & Ors [2016] EWHC 73 (Admin) (21 January 2016) URL: http://www.bailii.org/ew/cases/EWHC/Admin/2016/73.html para 29

5 Kebbell Developments Ltd, R (on the application of) v Leeds City Council & Anor [2016] EWHC 2664 (Admin)
URL: *http://www.bailii.org/ew/cases/EWHC/Admin/2016/2664.html*

evant development plan policies if there were in reality no such policies in place.

In the *Gladman* case referred to above Mr Justice Lewis approved this approach ruling that "neighbourhood development plan policies do not become, and do not have effect as if they were, strategic policies in a development plan document simply because there is, as yet, no development plan document in existence providing policies in relation to those aspects of the use and development of land."[6] In *DLA Delivery*[7] this approach was confirmed and reinforced by the Court of Appeal with Lord Justice Lindblom confirming that the "essential purpose" of this condition was to "ensure an appropriate degree of consistency between a neighbourhood development plan and the strategy of the extant, statutorily adopted development plan."

Condition f): EU Obligations

Condition (f) does not define "EU Obligations", which is unfortunate as this condition requires demonstrable compliance with a range of specific procedural requirements.

The NPPG[8] advises that the that the most relevant EU obligations in relation to neighbourhood plans are Directive 2001/42/EC – the SEA Directive[9], Directive 92/43/EEC – the Habitats Directive and Directive 2009/147/EC – the Birds Directive.

6 Gladman Developments Ltd, R (on the application of) v Aylesbury Vale District Council & Ors [2014] EWHC 4323 (Admin) para 58, 60 URL: http://www.bailii.org/ew/cases/EWHC/Admin/2014/4323.html Para 74

7 DLA Delivery Ltd, R (On the Application Of) v Lewes District Council [2017] EWCA Civ 58 (10 February 2017)
URL: *http://www.bailii.org/ew/cases/EWCA/Civ/2017/58.html*

8 Paragraph: 078 Reference ID: 41-078-20140306

- Demonstrating compliance with the SEA Directive is a requirement for all neighbourhood plans. Meeting this element of the basic condition relies primarily on the scope and content of the Environmental Report considered in detail above. It will be sensible for any qualifying body to discuss both considerations with the local authority well in advance of formal submission and to take formal advice if considerations within the scope of the relevant Directives emerge.

- Compliance with the other two Directives very much depends on the area in question and whether it is protected by either designation. The Habitats Directive establishes a European network of areas where the land in question is recognised as ecologically valuable and is safeguarded against potentially damaging developments[10]. The Birds Directive establishes a similar European network of special Protection Areas to guard against habitat loss and degradation that could threaten the conservation of wild birds[11]. It is important to find out whether part or whole of the designated area is affected by such a designation at an early stage and to ensure that any designation-specific requirements are complied with.

The NPPG goes on to state that "Other European directives, such as the Waste Framework Directive (2008/98/EC), Air Quality Directive (2008/50/EC) or the Water Framework Directive (2000/60/EC) may apply to the particular circumstances". Early

9 Directive 2001/42/EC

10 Council Directive 92/43/EEC

11 Directive 2009/147/EC

discussions with the local authority should clarify which apply to particular areas of land.

Human Rights and Equalities

There are two further 'EU obligations' that, though not mentioned in the NPPG, are relevant to the NDP process.

Cases such as *Buckley*[12] *Varey*[13] and *Chapman*[14] have already established that human rights considerations such as Article 1 of the First Protocol (the protection of property) and Article 8 (the right to respect for private and family life) must be taken into account in planning decisions – and the issue has already arisen in the context of NDPs in the case of RLT Built Environment v Cornwall Council[15]. The case concerned the proposal in a neighbourhood plan to impose a policy restriction on second homes and whether this was in compliance with Article 8. It was argued that such a policy could in the future result in article 8 rights being engaged in the future and so the council should have provided more justification than it had. Mr Justice Hickinbottom did not agree. He warned that the impact of the policy should not be overstated, and that if Article 8 were engaged in the future, there were sufficient checks in place to control its impact so the policy was sufficiently justified in Article 8 terms.

12 *Buckley v United Kingdom* app no 20348/92 [1996] ECHR 39

13 *Varey v United Kingdom* app no 26662/95 [2000] ECHR 692

14 *Chapman v United Kingdom* app no 27238/95 [2001] ECHR 43

15 R (RLT Built Environment) v The Cornwall Council & Anor, Court of Appeal – Administrative Court, November 10, 2016, [2016] EWHC 2817 (Admin)

The final overarching obligation to be considered is the Public Sector Equality Duty. Introduced by section 149 of the 2010 Equality Act, it requires public bodies to have due regard to the needs of members of the population who have a protected status when exercising any public function. Its relevance to planning cases was established in *Harris*[16] and explored in detail in *Coleman*[17] where claims established that a lack of proper regard to the particular needs of specific communities in the determination of planning applications, resulted in a breach of the Equality Act and led to the permissions being quashed. Although not yet tested in the context of NDPs it is clearly relevant to any plan that has positive or negative impacts on people in the community with protected characteristics of age, disability, gender reassignment, marriage and civil partnership, pregnancy and maternity, race, religion or belief, sex and sexual orientation. There is no formal requirement for showing that the duty has been met; though Equalities Impact Assessments are the usual way this is achieved, but it should not be forgotten.

---

16 Harris, R (on the application of) v The London Borough of Haringey [2010] EWCA Civ 703

17 Coleman, R (on the application of) v The London Borough of Barnet Council & Ors [2012] EWHC 3725

PART SIX

Examiner Report

As with other elements of the neighbourhood plan process, the scope of what the examiner may consider, and his or her powers in relation to it, are significantly restricted compared to the scope allowed for traditional development plans. It is not the role either of the Examiner or the local planning authority. It is not the role of either body to decide what the correct planning policies should be nor are they entitled to amend the plan to put it in a form which they would have written.

Paragraph 8 (1) of Schedule 4B lists the matters he must consider, including:

- Whether the draft neighbourhood development order meets the basic conditions.
- Whether the draft order complies with sections 61E(2), 61J and 61L.
- Whether the area for any referendum should extend beyond the neighbourhood area to which the draft order relates.

The examiner is expressly prohibited from considering any matter which does not fall into those listed apart from considering whether the draft neighbourhood plan is compatible with human rights.[1]

1 Town and Country Planning Act 1990, Sch 4B, para 8(6) as applied to neighbourhood plans by the Planning and Compulsory Purchase Act 2004, s 38C.

Once the examination is completed, the examiner will prepare a formal report for publication. The content of that report is also constrained by paragraph 10 of Schedule 4B to the 1990 Act as it can only recommend:

- that the draft plan is submitted to a referendum; or
- that modifications specified in the report are made to the draft plan and that the draft plan as modified is submitted to a referendum; or
- that the proposal for the [plan] is refused.

The power to make modifications is set out in paragraph 10 of the Schedule. The modifications must be:

- modifications that the examiner considers need to be made to secure that the draft plan meets the basic conditions mentioned in paragraph 8(2);
- modifications that the examiner considers need to be made to secure that the draft plan complies with the provision made by or under sections 38A and 38B of the 2004 Act; or
- modifications for the purpose of correcting errors.

The report must give reasons for each of its recommendations, and contain a summary of its main findings.

The *Legard* [2] case centred around the designation of a parcel of land as a "Local Green Space", as defined by paragraph 77 of the Framework and considered the role of the Examiner in some detail. It was claimed that the Examiner failed to understand and apply the Framework policy correctly, and that his reasons were inadequate, in that they failed to adequately explain why he had concluded that the designation should apply, and further failed to engage with the fact that the site had a lawful use as a consequence of being used for commercial purposes associated with storage and horticulture as well as being used primarily as contractor's stores.

Mr Justice Dove considered all of the issues raised in detail. First, he confirmed that there was no defect in the way in which paragraph 77 was interpreted "the interpretation of paragraph 77 of the Framework deployed by the Examiner is the interpretation which is to be preferred". He went on to consider and confirm the formal requirements relating to the standard and content of the Examiner's reasons and how they should be properly observed. Mr Justic Dove considered a number of cases in this context[3], and formally affirmed the principles set out by Mrs Justice Lang in *Bewley Homes*[4] where Mrs Justice Lang specifically contrasted the standard expected of an Inspector when deciding a planning appeal with those required of an examiner:

- the Examiner will not consider whether a neighbourhood plan meets the requirements of "soundness" in NPPF 182...(47)

---

2 Legard, R (On the Application Of) v The Royal Borough of Kensington and Chelsea [2018] EWHC 32 (Admin)

3 (Crown Hall Estates Ltd) v Chichester District Council [2016] EWHC 73 and R(Swan Quay LLP) v Swale Borough Council [2017] EWHC 420,

4 R(Bewley Homes PLC) v Waverley Borough Council [2017] EWHC 1776.

- … the Examiner will not embark upon the type of detailed scrutiny of the draft policies and the relevant evidence which is conducted by an Inspector when examining a draft Local Plan(48)

- …The Inspector is only required to give reasons for his recommendations, which are themselves limited to one of the three options in paragraph 10(2). (51)

- This limited duty may be contrasted with the broad duty imposed upon Inspectors under the Town and Country Planning Appeals (Determination by Inspectors) (Inquiries Procedure)(England) Rules 2000 (52).

Mr Justice Dove agreed with this distinction and ruled that "In testing whether or not the Examiners reasons are legally adequate it is important to focus upon such reasons as are necessary to explain the report's recommendations, and to bear in mind that in respect of the main findings of the report the duty is simply to provide a summary. In respect of the reasons provided they will of course have to be intelligible and explain why the recommendation has been reached, but they do not have to refer to every matter raised in the context of the debate, solely the principal controversial issues." He concluded that "I am satisfied that the Examiner's reasons were clear and adequate, and further that the conclusions which he reached were arrived at following a proper interpretation of paragraph 77 of the Framework.

Bias

The issue of examiners' bias has emerged as a ground of challenge in a number of cases, including *Legard*[5], so is worth considering at this point. The *Legard*[6] decision is particularly useful as Mr Justice Dove included a comprehensive overview of the existing case law on this issue, which is worth summarising here:

- The legal principles are established in *Porter v Magill*[7] : whether the fair-minded and informed observer, having considered the facts, would conclude that there was a real possibility that the tribunal was biased.
- There were a number of cases in the 1980s relating to the conduct of planning inspectors during the course of an appeal listed and considered in the judgment.[8]
- More recent cases on the conduct of members of planning committees including *Georgiou,*[9] *Island Farm*[10] and *Lewis*[11]

5 BDW Trading Ltd (t/a Barratt Homes) & Anor v Cheshire West & Chester Borough Council & Ors [2014] EWHC 1470 (Admin) and DLA Delivery Ltd, R (On the Application Of) v Lewes District Council [2017] EWCA Civ 58

6 Legard, R (On the Application Of) v The Royal Borough of Kensington and Chelsea [2018] EWHC 32

7 Porter v Magill [2001] UKHL 67; [2002] 2 AC 357.

8 Furmston v Secretary of State for the Environment [1982] JPL 49, Simmons v Secretary of State for the Environment [1985] JPL 49, British Muslims Association v Secretary of State for the Environment [1988] 55 PCR 205, Cotterell v Secretary of State for the Environment [1991] 2 PLR 3

9 Georgiou v London Borough of Enfield and others [2004] EWHC 779.

10 R(on the application of Island Farm Development Ltd) v Bridgend County Borough Council [2007] LGR 60

11 R(Lewis) v Redcar and Cleveland Borough Council [2008] EWCA Civ 746; [2009] 1 WLR 83

were also summarised along with the 2016 *Broadview*[12] case that considered, among other things, conversations in the House of Commons tea room.

Mr Justice Dove then went on to set out the principles that should apply to answering the fundamental question: whether a fair-minded and informed observer, having considered those facts, would conclude that there was a real possibility of bias on behalf of the decision-maker. He described the fair-minded observer as "neither unduly suspicious nor complacent" who would "take account of the overall context". He also acknowledged that members of local authorities "will have political allegiances and policy positions" or even "a predisposition in relation to a particular decision" but that would not amount to predetermination provided they approach the decision "with a mind which is willing to grasp all of the merits to be considered, and which is not closed". He concluded that in the particular circumstances of that case there was "neither apparent bias nor unfairness in the defendant's involvement in the making of the Neighbourhood Plan".

Council Decision on Report

Once the report is received, the local authority must:

- Arrange for the publication of the report in such manner as may be prescribed (Paragraph 10(8) of Schedule 4B).
- Consider, and decide what action to take in response to, each of the recommendations made: (Paragraph 12).

12 Broadview Energy Developments v Secretary of State for Communities and Local Government and others [2016] EWCA Civ 562.

- Comply with the relevant requirements in Regulation 17 and 17A.

The local authority may modify the plan (Paragraph 12 (6)) but if they are for the purpose of correcting errors or necessary to ensure:

- That the draft plan meets the basic conditions.
- That the draft plan is compatible with the Convention rights.
- That the draft plan complies with sections 61E(2), 61J and 61L.

The local authority may also make a decision that differs from the examiner's recommendation (Schedule 4B paragraph 13). If the reason for the difference is due to the receipt of new evidence or a new fact or a different view as to a particular fact, they must notify certain persons (prescribed by Regulation 17A) of the proposed decision (and the reason for it) and invite representations. They may also refer the issue back for independent examination. Regulation 17A additionally imposes strict time limits on either process.

Regulation 18 requires that when the local authority has decided what action to take in response to the recommendations of an examiner and/or what modifications, if any, they are to make to the draft plan or to extend the area to which the referendum is (or referendums are) to take place; or that they are not satisfied with the plan proposal they must, as soon as possible afterwards, publish the decision and their reasons for it, details of where and when the decision statement may be inspected; and the examiner's report.

Referendum

If the local authority is satisfied that the proposed plan meets the basic conditions and is compatible with the Convention rights then a referendum "must be held" on the draft plan (Schedule 4B paragraph 14. The plan cannot be made unless at least half of the people voting vote in favour of it.

The requirements are set out in paragraphs 14, 15 and 16 of Schedule 4B and the 2012 Regulations. Paragraph 14 requires the local authority to 'make arrangements' for the referendum to take place in the referendum area. Anyone can vote if they are already registered as a voter, and they live in the referendum area. Paragraph 15 sets out provision in relation to additional referendums held in a designated business area and Paragraph 16 provides for Regulations to be made – in this case the Neighbourhood Planning (Referendums) Regulations 2012 (the "Referendum Regulations".[13])

The Referendum Regulations provide detailed guidance on the way in which neighbourhood plan referenda must be carried out and are based upon the Local Authorities (Conduct of Referendums) (England) Regulations 2012. The main requirements can be summarised as follows:

- Regulation 3 and Schedule 1 prescribe the form of words of the question to be asked in a referendum. There are 3 questions depending on whether the referendum relates to a neighbourhood development plan, a neighbourhood development order or a community right to build order. For a neighbourhood plan the question is "Do you want [*insert name of local planning authority*] to use the neigh-

13 SI 2012/2031

bourhood plan for [*insert name of neighbourhood area*] to help it decide planning applications in the neighbourhood area?"

- Regulation 4 provides that the relevant council responsible for the referendum must publish a detailed notice of the referendum in its local area at least 28 working days before the date of the referendum. It also provides for weekends, bank holidays and public holidays to be ignored in calculating certain periods of time for the referendum period. This is to ensure people living in the local authority's area are aware that a referendum is due to be held, the subject matter of that referendum and that they are informed of key information relating to the referendum.

- Regulation 5 imposes restrictions on the material that may be published, displayed or distributed by and on behalf of the authority in the period beginning 28 working days before the date of the referendum to ensure the local authority is not able to unduly influence the result of the referendum.

- Regulation 6 prescribes a limit on campaign expenses. Schedule 2 makes provision about the matters relevant to referendum expenses. Regulation 6(3) includes an offence for a campaign organiser to knowingly incur expenses expenditure in excess of the referendum expenses limit.

- Regulation 7 provides that where certain property, services and facilities are used free of charge or at a significant discount then where the cost is greater than £200 the full cost of that use will be treated as incurred by way of referendum expenses for the purposes of regulation 6.

- Regulation 8 provides for the conduct of a referendum which is not combined with any other polls.

- Regulation 9 specifies who is to be the counting officer at the referendum.

- Regulation 10 provides that where the referendum area includes any part of the area of more than one council, the authorities must appoint a person to be the Chief Counting Officer for the cross boundary referendum. This person will have a power of direction over counting officers in each relevant council's area, including the power to order a re-count.

- Regulation 11 makes provision for the conduct of referendums when combined with the poll at elections. Where a "relevant election" is due to be held up to 28 days after a neighbourhood planning referendum is due to be held, the neighbourhood planning referendum may be held on the same date, regulated by the Neighbourhood Planning Referendums (Combination of Polls) Rules in Schedule 5.

- Regulation 12 applies other electoral legislation to facilitate the conduct of such referendums.

- Regulation 13 makes provision as to the modification of election rules in relation to the relevant election with which the referendum is combined.

- Regulation 14 exempts advertisements relating specifically to the referendum from regulations under the 1990 Act controlling the display of advertisements.

- Regulation 15 provides that premises used in relation to the referendum for public meetings or the taking of the poll are to be treated as unoccupied for rating purposes.

- Regulation 16 allows for the circumstances where the relevant council for a referendum is not the local planning authority.

There have been no issues to date with the practical arrangements for such process and no case law relating to this aspect of the process.

Adoption

Section 38 A (4)(b) provides that the neighbourhood plan 'must be made' if more than half of those voting have voted in favour of the plan. Section 38A(4) of the 2004 Act also requires that the relevant local planning authority must make the plan as soon as reasonably practicable after the referendum is held or "by such date as may be prescribed." Regulation 18A requires that the plan must be made no later than 8 weeks beginning with the day immediately following that on which the last applicable referendum is held.

The process is set out in regulations 19, 20 and 18A of the General Regulations 2012:

- Regulation 19 requires that as soon as possible after deciding to make a neighbourhood development plan under section 38A(4) of the 2004 Act or refusing to make a plan under section 38A(6) of the 2004 Act, a local planning authority must—

- o publish on their website and in such other manner as they consider is likely to bring the decision to the attention of people who live, work or carry on business in the neighbourhood area—a statement setting out the decision and their reasons for making that decision ("the decision statement"); details of where and when the decision statement may be inspected; and

- o send a copy of the decision statement to— (i) the qualifying body; and (ii) any person who asked to be notified of the decision.

Regulation 19 additionally requires that as soon as possible after deciding to make or refusing to make a neighbourhood plan a local planning authority must:

- publish on their website and in such other manner as they consider is likely to bring the decision to the attention of people who live, work or carry on business in the neighbourhood area-a statement setting out the decision and their reasons for making that decision and details of where and when the decision statement may be inspected; and

- send a copy of the decision statement to the qualifying body; and any person who asked to be notified of the decision.

Regulation 20 requires that as soon as possible after making a neighbourhood development plan under section 38A(4) of the 2004 Act, a local planning authority must publish on their website and in such other manner as they consider is likely to bring the decision to the attention of people who live, work or carry on business in the neighbourhood area:

- the neighbourhood development plan;
- details of where and when the neighbourhood development plan may be inspected;
- notify any person who asked to be notified of the making of the neighbourhood development plan that it has been made and where and when it may be inspected.

The plan has legal effect as soon as it is made by the local planning authority and has statutory force in the determination of any relevant planning proposal from that date onwards.

Review and Modification

Developing embryonic policies into an adopted document with development plan status is a real achievement but is not the end of the plan process. The planning system is a reflection of the society it seeks to regulate and so long as society remains an evolving and dynamic entity, so will its plans. In addition, as shown above, as soon as any development plan becomes "out of date" its policies will have less weight against other, more recently adopted plans. Finally, in the absence of an up to date plan, the presumption in favour of sustainable development will come into force. If the neighbourhood plan is to continue to be relevant to its local area, and play an influential role in local development proposals, it must evolve to fit its context.

This is no easy task. The Framework itself is currently under review and a new Framework is likely to be introduced in the summer of 2018. The NPPG is an online, organic document that is constantly being reviewed and changed. The Government may also make quite sweeping changes to national planning policy with a simple written ministerial statement and need neither forewarn or consult on such changes[14]. Each and every neighbourhood plan is required to be 'in conformity with' superior plans produced by relevant local planning authorities so each time one of these authorities adopts a superior plan there is a risk that conformity is lost in the process. The neighbourhood plan does not lose its status, but the weight of its policies will be significantly diminished.

The provisions for revocation and modification of neighbourhood plans are contained in by section 61M of the 1990 Planning Act. The power to revoke a plan is primarily with the Secretary of State though the local planning authority may revoke the plan themselves if the Secretary of State consents and in either case reasons must be given. The local planning authority is also empowered to modify plans, through replacing the order with a new one containing the modification.

This power was extended by section 4 of the Neighbourhood Planning Act 2017 which made changes to section 61M of the 1990 Act and introduced a new Schedule 2A of the 2004 Act. The primary change is to allow modification of a neighbourhood plan if the local authority considers that the modification does not materially affect the policies in the plan, with Schedule 2A setting out the new new procedure for modification of neighbourhood development plans in these circumstances as follows:

---

14 Richborough Estates Ltd v Secretary of State for Housing, Communities And Local Government [2018] EWHC 33 (Admin)

- The qualifying body submits the proposal accompanied by the modified draft of the plan and a statement containing a summary of the proposals and sets out reasons why the plan should be modified as proposed.

- The local authority must give appropriate advice and assistance to facilitate the development of a proposal but they have no duty to give financial assistance.

- The proposal must be made in a 'prescribed form' and accompanied by 'prescribed documents'.

- All 'prescribed persons must be sent a copy of the proposal, the draft plan and relevant documents.

- It must also be compliant with any 'standards' set by the Secretary of State.

The local authority can refuse to consider the proposals - by notifying the qualifying body and giving reasons for the decision – if they believe that they are a repeat proposal. The local authority can also refuse to consider the proposal if they are not satisfied that:

- The qualifying body is authorised.

- The proposal complies with the requirements of Section 61M of the 1990 Act, Sections 38A and 38B and paragraph 1 of Schedule A2 and any relevant regulations.

If the local authority considers that the modification should be made, but considers that the modifications "are so significant or substantial as to change the nature of the neighbourhood development plan which the draft plan would replace" they must instead consider the proposal under Schedule 4B of the 1990 Act.

If the Council wants to proceed on a 'streamlined' basis they must appoint an examiner (who may be the employee of another local authority) in consultation and agreement with the qualifying body and submit the modified plan for independent examination and make appropriate arrangements for that examination.

- The examination must be in public but will generally be considered through written representations though an oral hearing may be convened if there are "exceptional reasons for doing so"

- The examiner will consider firstly whether the modifications "are so significant or substantial as to change the nature of the neighbourhood development plan which the draft plan would replace." If this is the case then the examiner must notify the qualifying body and the local planning authority, with reasons. The qualifying body can proceed but the plan will be considered under Schedule 4B.

- Otherwise, the examiner must consider whether the draft plan complies with the basic conditions and "such other matters as may be prescribed".

- The examiner must report on the plan following examination and the report must recommend that the plan should be 1) made as submitted 2) made with modifications 3) not made. Modifications can only made to secure compliance with the basic conditions, Human Rights, sections 38A and 38B and correcting areas. Reasons must be given and a copy sent to the qualifying body and the local planning authority.

- The local authority must publicise the report and make the draft plan as soon as reasonably practicable, including recommended modifications unless they consider that it would breach, or would otherwise be incompatible with, any EU obligation or any of the Convention rights, in which case they can either not make the plan – and give reasons why not, or make the draft plan with modification must give reasons "to secure that the draft plan is compatible with EU obligations and the Convention rights".
- The authority must make the draft plan s soon as reasonably practicable and, in any event, by such date as may be prescribed. The qualifying body can withdraw the proposal before any action is taken on it but the proposal will remain valid if it has already gone to an examiner.

The new process is certainly quicker because it potentially reduces the scope of the matters considered by the Qualifying Body, the Local Authority and the Examiner and also because it removes the need for a referendum – and the cost and time that this involves. Removal of the referendum stage will also remove at least one opportunity for a third-party challenge. However, the process is as yet untested and there is ample scope for challenges to be made based on the interpretation of terms such as 'materially affect'.

So far, Schedule 2A has been brought into force but no regulations have been made. However, for the qualifying body who wants to ensure that their plan remains effective, and for the local authority that wants to ensure that the modification is smooth and as free from the risk of challenge as possible, it makes sense to treat the made plan as an organic document, through an ongoing review of its content including notes of amendments that need to be made, including minor issues such as typographical errors.

Attention will need to be paid on an ongoing basis to policies that might need to be amended if either national policy or the strategic policies in local plans are about to change. The emerging national planning policy framework includes a defined list of policies that may provide a specific reason for restricting development including land designated as Local Green Space and irreplaceable habitats including ancient woodland; aged or veteran trees. A qualifying body might want to take advantage of this to include new protective policies for local green spaces or valuable trees. And now that there is a legal duty to review a plan every five years, the qualifying body may want to work with the local authority and ensure that its review dovetails with that of the local authority.

PART SEVEN

So far this book has set the neighbourhood plan process in its legal and policy context and examined the whole plan process in detail. This section summarises the the interrelationship of neighbourhood plans – once adopted – with the way in which Community Infrastructure Levy is collected and applied, sets out the ways in which all parties to the neighbourhood plan process can benefit from a cooperative approach and ends with some reflections on the past, present and future position of neighbourhood plans in the current system.

CIL – Legal Principles

For as long as local authorities have been granting planning permission for land, they have also wrestled with the issue of assessing the 'cost' of a development on the land and its community, and how to secure some kind of compensation for that cost from the owner or developer benefitting from the consent.

Traditionally, this issue was dealt with through planning agreements negotiated and completed in parallel with the grant of a consent, ensuring that if the development went ahead, various public benefits would be secured in parallel with it. These are still in force and are generally referred to as 'section 106' or 'planning obligation' agreements. They are entered into between the owner of the land and the local planning authority and secure a range of benefits in cash or kind. Financial payments may be made to local transport, education and health providers, or there may be more tangible benefits such as affordable housing or the provision of new roads, schools and social facilities.

Theoretically, the purpose of a section 106 agreement is to "outweigh the disbenefit" of a particular development proposal and originally, the tests for validity of section 106 agreements were set in planning policy. The lack of specific legal requirements or rigorous policy guidance led to a wide diversity of approaches, leading to developers complaining about excessive local authority "shopping lists" and communities alleging that permissions were available for those developers who could afford to 'buy' them with an attractive range of planning benefits.

Part 11 of the Planning Act 2008 introduced the notion of a "Community Infrastructure Levy" - a charge based on the area of new space generated by development that would pay for a limited range of strategic infrastructure to support the development of an area generally. Local authorities were given discretion to set their own charge per square metre and to charge different rates for different uses in different areas. It was brought into force on 6 April 2010 by the Community Infrastructure Levy Regulations 2010[1], made under section 206 of the 2008 Act. The 2010 Regulations did not replace the current system of 106 obligations but they did set legal restrictions on what they could be secured for and applied to.

CIL and Neighbourhood Plans

Section 115 of the Localism Act 2011 inserted new sections 216A and 216B into the 2008 Act, creating a new power for regulations to be made requiring authorities collecting CIL to pass funds to other bodies, including areas with an adopted neighbourhood development plan. The government's reasoning was set out as follows: "We are requiring a larger, and uncapped, amount to be

1 http://www.legislation.gov.uk/uksi/2010/948/contents/made

passed to areas with a Neighbourhood Development Plan in place because they have embraced positive planning for future development in their local area...This both rewards and incentivises neighbourhood planning. Neighbourhoods that have organised themselves to bring forward a plan or order are already positively engaged with the planning process, so it is right they are given more control over this aspect of planning for development. Offering a greater incentive for neighbourhoods taking a proactive approach to planning by adopting neighbourhood plans and orders should also help nudge others in this direction."[2]

The Community Infrastructure Levy (Amendment) regulations were made in 2013 and introduced new regulations 58A, 59A to 59F and 62A into the Community Infrastructure Levy Regulations. The overall effect of these new regulations is to require local authorities to pass on 25% of any CIL receipts to areas with a Neighbourhood Development plan in place, in proportion to the amount of new development in that area. This is a valuable source of potential local income.

It has taken time for CIL to be introduced and there are few areas where there is both an adopted plan and a CIL regime in place. The Regulations are therefore largely untested but it is still worth being aware of the most useful provisions:

- Regulation 58A defines a number of terms including "CIL expenditure", "CIL receipts" and "neighbourhood development plan" and clarifies indexation provisions.

- Regulation 59A introduces a new duty on local authorities to pass CIL to local councils, stating specifically that "a charging authority...must pass to every local council

2 http://www.legislation.gov.uk/uksi/2013/982/pdfs/uksiem_20130982_en.pdf

within its area a proportion of CIL receipts calculated in accordance with this regulation.

- Regulation 59A also sets the level as 25% "where all or part of a chargeable development is within an area that has a neighbourhood development plan in place" and then goes on to specify that "in place" means that the neighbourhood development plan has been made and is "extant in relation to the relevant area on the day when planning permission first permits that development."
- Regulation 59B includes within the 25% a proportion of the value of any land transferred instead of a CIL payment.

Regulation 59C specifies what the 'neighbourhood portion' can be spent on, once transferred. This is important because the spending powers of local bodies are wider than those of local authorities. Local authorities must apply CIL to "funding the provision, improvement, replacement, operation or maintenance of infrastructure to support the development of its area." In terms of the neighbourhood portion the power is wider so CIL revenues can be used to fund "anything else that is concerned with addressing the demands that development places on an area." This is a very wide power indeed and the Explanatory Note to the Regulations acknowledges that it "gives parish and community councils greater freedom over what to spend the neighbourhood funding element on. These wider spending powers are important because they allow the community to decide what they need to help mitigate the impact of development."

Regulation 59D sets out the payment periods associated with the neighbourhood funds that are passed directly to parish and community councils. The charging authority and the parish or community council have the freedom to set their own timetable for payments. However, where they do not have an agreement in place these regulations set out a default timetable as follows:

- The charging authority must make payment in respect of the CIL it receives from 1st April to 30th September in any financial year to the local body by 28th October of that financial year.

- The charging authority must make payment in respect of the CIL it receives from 1st October to 31st March in any financial year to the local body by 28th April of the following financial year.

The government's purpose is acknowledged as being "to ensure that payments are made in a timely manner". However, the regulations also provide for situations where the funds have not been spent within 5 years of being transferred or have been used for another purpose. In this situation Regulation 59E provides for the recovery of the funds by the charging authority through service of a notice on the local body requiring it to repay some or all of the CIL receipts that the regulation refers to. The notice must specify the amount of CIL receipts to be repaid; the reasons for requiring those receipts to be repaid; and the date by which repayment is to be made (allowing at least 28 days for this). If the full amount is not recovered, the balance can be taken from future receipts.

Finally, regulation 62A introduces arrangements for reporting by parish and community councils. They must publish each year their total CIL receipts and expenditure, a summary of things to which the Levy has been applied and the levy expenditure on each; and the total amount of Levy receipts retained at the end of the reported year from that year and previous years.

As well as changes to the law, the Government has issued guidance on the neighbourhood portion as part of the wider online National Planning Policy Guidance and two elements of this are worth noting. First, the guidance is also clear that funding can be spent "on a wider range of things than the rest of the levy, provided that it meets the requirement to 'support the development of the area' and include affordable housing, which is specifically excluded from CIL spending by a local authority[3]. The NPPG advises that the local authority should:

- Engage with the community and be clear on what their approach to engagement will be.
- Agree with the community how best to spend the funding.
- Ensure that the funding matches priorities expressed by local communities.
- Consider phasing of developments, the costs of different projects and their importance.
- Consider how the funding can be used to deliver infrastructure identified in the plan.

This is helpful guidance but is not legally enforceable. For the local planning forum that has not been able to establish or maintain a good working relationship with the local authority, they will be faced with the frustrating situation of being entitled to 25% of the CIL receipts for the area, but without very much power or influence in the way those funds are spent. This is just one reason why it is well worth considering, right from the start of the process, an application to become a parish council.

3 Paragraph: 078 Reference ID: 25-078-20140612

For the parish, town or community council that has actually received the relevant funding, the guidance reminds them that they are already under a legal duty to "make arrangements for the proper administration of their financial affairs" and have "systems in place to ensure effective financial control". [4] The guidance reminds these bodies of their responsibilities under Regulation 62A, stating that there is no prescribed format but that it must be included in the overall published accounts.[5]

Working With the Local Authority

It should be clear from this book that the local authority for the area where the plan is situated will play an essential role in the development and adoption of a neighbourhood plan. Some of the arrangements are required by the law:

- *S*chedule 4B of the 1990 Act includes, at Paragraph 3, a duty on local planning authorities to provide advice and assistance to qualifying bodies in development proposals for plans or orders, including providing technical advice on how to draw up an order or plan or facilitating consultation with the public on proposals.

- Section 2 of the 2017 Act amends Schedule 1 of the 1990 Act to require a local planning authority or the Secretary of State to automatically notify qualifying bodies of any future planning applications or alterations to those applications in the relevant neighbourhood area, where there is an advanced neighbourhood plan and the qualifying body has

4 Section 1515 Local Government Act 1972, Accounts and Audit (England) Regulations 2011

5 Paragraph: 080 Reference ID: 25-080-20140612

not confirmed in writing to the local planning authority that it does not wish to be notified.

- Section 6 of the 2017 Act amends section 18 of the 2004 Act, adding to the existing duty to prepare a statement of community involvement setting out the authority's policy for involving interested parties in the preparation of local development documents an additional duty to give advice or assistance to qualifying bodies to facilitate proposals for neighbourhood development plans (including proposals for the modification of neighbourhood development plans) or orders.

These provisions provide qualifying bodies with blunt legal tools to that can be asserted where a local authority is delaying the plan process, but it is much better if the two bodies can find a way to work together on the production and adoption of a plan from the start. The main reason for this is the need to work together in the event of a third-party challenge. Section 61N of the 1990 Act anticipates a number of decisions that may be challenged:

- A decision to act under section 61E(4) or (8) (making a neighbourhood plan.
- A decision under paragraph 12 of Schedule 4B (consideration by local planning authority of recommendations made by examiner).
- Anything relating to a referendum under paragraph 14 or 15 of Schedule 4B .

In each case, the validity of the plan itself will be at stake but it is the local authority and not the qualifying body which must respond to the challenge – the two parties may find themselves needing to act together and quickly – this will be much easier if relations are established and friendly.

Each planning authority, and each NDP is different so the approach taken will change from area to area but there are a number of ways in which cooperation can be achieved that is common to all.

- Regulation 14 requires the qualifying body to send a copy of the proposals for a neighbourhood development plan to the local planning authority but this should not be the first time that the local authority has seen the plan. Even if the parties disagree about the content of the policies, both should at least be aware of what those policies are and any amendments that have been made, at the time those policies are drafted or amended.

- Relevant officers and members should be identified early in the process. Ideally this should include key officers involved with setting committee dates and organising elections as well as planning policy operatives as this will help to avoid delays on getting decisions on the right meeting agenda at the right time and smooth the referendum process.

- Regular meetings between officers and the individuals making the plan will help focus attention on progress and help to establish a cooperative relationship.

- The relevant officers should be regularly invited to public meetings concerning the plan process.

- Ideally, project plans, checklists and timetables should be agreed with the Council at the start of the process and reviewed regularly.

Final Thoughts

The introduction to this book outlined the political and legislative origins of the Neighbourhood Plan – introduced by the Coalition government from a resolutely positive perspective. However, even before neighbourhood plans became a legislative possibility, property professionals were querying how they would integrate with the current system. In 2010, Liz Peace, chief executive of the British Property Federation, raised concerns including what status the plans would have and how they would interrelate with existing plans[6] while the British Council of Shopping Centres executive director Edward Cooke anticipated that neighbourhood planning could facilitate an increase in opposition to new development. [7]

Another issue raised very early in the process was how democratic these plans would be in practice. In 2010 Friends of the Earth's planning campaigner Anna Watson said: "If localism is to thrive more must be done to allow people to participate fairly in the planning process – these Government plans could create a postcode lottery, two-tier planning system, where cash-strapped communities struggle to make their voices heard."[8] In addition, there were academics who criticised the system as creating "an

6 BPF Press Release, Property industry welcomes publication of Localism Bill, 13 December 2010

7 BCSC Press Release, BSCS: Localism must not hinder property-led regeneration, 13 December 2010

8 Friends of the Earth Press Release, Localism Bill fails vital green test, 13 December 2010

uneven geography of representation in favour of the better educated, well-off and more vocal social groups".[9]

Neighbourhood plans have certainly proved more disruptive than expected. The neighbourhood plan has development plan status once adopted but it is quicker and easier to adopt than a traditional local plan. In areas where the local plan process is mired in delay and arguments over housing supply, the neighbourhood plan is the only up to date development plan in place. There has been significant caselaw on the interrelationship between neighbourhood and other development plans, and developer proposals, and most have been resolved in favour of the neighbourhood plan.

Neighbourhood plans may not be as equitable as their promoters believed them to be. It is not the role of this book to consider the interrelationship between the likelihood of a plan being adopted and the socioeconomic status of the community but it does seem as though they have proliferated in areas of relative affluence where there is a community with the necessary time and resources available. As Teresa Pearce MP pointed out in the debate on the Neighbourhood Planning Bill in October 2016: "councils receive £5,000 for each neighbourhood plan area designated, and £20,000 for each neighbourhood plan referendum, but… costs can exceed the moneys that the council receives…neighbourhood planning must be open to all, and disadvantaged communities need to be able to participate."[10]

Finally, some communities have found themselves disappointed even where plans have been adopted. As the NPPG recognises, where there is conflict between one plan and another: "conflict

9 Simin Davoudi & Paul Cowie 'Are English Neighbourhood forums democratically legitimate?' Planning Theory and Practice Vol 1 No. 4 562

10 10 October 2016 Volume 615 column 85

must be resolved by the decision maker favouring the policy which is contained in the last document to become part of the development plan."[11] A community can then work hard to get its plan adopted, only to find key policies outweighed in the application process for the subsequent adoption of conflicting policies in a superior plan.

Nevertheless, the number of plans is increasing exponentially. In September 2012 the Department for Communities and Local Government published its first "Notes on neighbourhood planning".[12] Edition 4 published announced the adoption of the first neighbourhood plan in Upper Eden in March 2013. The most recent edition of the 'Notes' recognised the 500th referendum in favour of adoption of a neighbourhood plan.[13]

Neighbourhood planning continues to be supported in both legislation and policy. On 31 July, section 13(2) of the Neighbourhood Planning Act 2017 comes into force requiring local planning authorities to set out their neighbourhood planning support in their 'Statement of Community Involvement'. [14] The draft revised National Planning Policy Framework[15]includes proposals include:

---

11 Paragraph: 009 Reference ID: 41-009-20160211

12 https://www.gov.uk/government/publications/notes-on-neighbourhood-planning-edition-1

13 https://www.gov.uk/government/publications/notes-on-neighbourhood-planning-edition-20

14 Regulation 4 of the Neighbourhood Planning Act 2017 (Commencement No.3) Regulations 2018

15 https://assets.publishing.service.gov.uk/government/uploads/system/uploads/attachment_data/file/685289/Draft_revised_National_Planning_Policy_Framework.pdf

- The protection of certain plans for two years after a plan is successful at referendum, where plans contain policies for housing and allocate sites for housing development to meet needs (para 12-14).

- The importance of neighbourhood plans in identifying the special qualities of each area and explaining how this should be reflected in development (paragraph 124).

- The potential for neighbourhood plans to alter Green Belt boundaries (paragraph 135).

The Government maintains a resolutely positive rhetoric on the subject. On 30th January 2018 Dominic Raab, the minister for housing, confirmed that "We will continue to protect neighbourhood plans in national policy, and decision takers—whether that is the local authority, the planning inspector or the Secretary of State himself—must respect that national policy." [16] and has supported the rhetoric with money – most recently a 23 million fund – being delivered by Locality and Groundwork to help local groups to develop a neighbourhood plan.[17]

In his seminal work that is widely accepted to set the foundations of planning in England[18] Eberneezer Howard argued that one of the most "pressing questions of the day" was "how to restore the people to the land — that beautiful land of ours, with its canopy of sky, the air that blows upon it, the sun that warms it." However disruptive and problematic it is, Neighbourhood Plans are cer-

16 Westminster Hall Debate "Town and Village Plans" 30 January 2018 column 338

17 https://www.gov.uk/government/news/government-commits-to-further-support-for-neighbourhood-planning

18 Ebeneezer Howard: *To-morrow: A Peaceful Path to Real Reform* (1898)

tainly playing their part in engaging with that question – and are unquestionably here to stay.

GLOSSARY

The 1990 Act	The Town and Country Planning Act 1990
The 2004 Act	The Planning and Compulsory Purchase Act 2004
The 2004 Regulations	Environmental Assessment of Plans and Programmes Regulations 2004
The 2012 Regulations	The Neighbourhood Planning (General) Regulations 2012
The Framework	2012 National Planning Policy Framework
NDP	Neighbourhood Development Plan
NPPG	National Planning Policy Guidance
The Referendum Regulations	The Neighbourhood Planning (Referendums) Regulations 2012

MORE BOOKS BY LAW BRIEF PUBLISHING

'Arguments and Tactics for Personal Injury and Clinical Negligence Claims' by Dorian Williams
'A Practical Guide to QOCS and Fundamental Dishonesty' by James Bentley
'A Practical Guide to Drone Law' by Rufus Ballaster, Andrew Firman, Eleanor Clot
'Practical Mediation: A Guide for Mediators, Advocates, Advisers, Lawyers, and Students in Civil, Commercial, Business, Property, Workplace, and Employment Cases' by Jonathan Dingle with John Sephton
'Practical Horse Law: A Guide for Owners and Riders' by Brenda Gilligan
'A Comparative Guide to Standard Form Construction and Engineering Contracts' by Jon Close
'A Practical Guide to Compliance for Personal Injury Firms Working With Claims Management Companies' by Paul Bennett
'A Practical Guide to the Landlord and Tenant Act 1954: Commercial Tenancies' by Richard Hayes & David Sawtell
'A Practical Guide to Personal Injury Claims Involving Animals' by Jonathan Hand
'A Practical Guide to Psychiatric Claims in Personal Injury' by Liam Ryan
'Introduction to the Law of Community Care in England and Wales' by Alan Robinson
'A Practical Guide to Dog Law for Owners and Others' by Andrea Pitt
'Ellis and Kevan on Credit Hire – 5th Edition' by Aidan Ellis & Tim Kevan
'RTA Allegations of Fraud in a Post-Jackson Era: The Handbook – 2nd Edition' by Andrew Mckie
'RTA Personal Injury Claims: A Practical Guide Post-Jackson' by Andrew Mckie
'On Experts: CPR35 for Lawyers and Experts' by David Boyle
'An Introduction to Personal Injury Law' by David Boyle
'A Practical Guide to Claims Arising From Accidents Abroad and Travel Claims' by Andrew Mckie & Ian Skeate
'A Practical Guide to Cosmetic Surgery Claims' by Dr Victoria Handley
'A Practical Guide to Chronic Pain Claims' by Pankaj Madan
'A Practical Guide to Claims Arising from Fatal Accidents' by James Patience

'A Practical Approach to Clinical Negligence Post-Jackson' by Geoffrey Simpson-Scott
'A Practical Guide to Personal Injury Trusts' by Alan Robinson
'Employers' Liability Claims: A Practical Guide Post-Jackson' by Andrew Mckie
'A Practical Guide to Subtle Brain Injury Claims' by Pankaj Madan
'The Law of Driverless Cars: An Introduction' by Alex Glassbrook
'A Practical Guide to Costs in Personal Injury Cases' by Matthew Hoe
'A Practical Guide to Alternative Dispute Resolution in Personal Injury Claims – Getting the Most Out of ADR Post-Jackson' by Peter Causton, Nichola Evans, James Arrowsmith
'A Practical Guide to Personal Injuries in Sport' by Adam Walker & Patricia Leonard
'The No Nonsense Solicitors' Practice: A Guide To Running Your Firm' by Bettina Brueggemann
'Baby Steps: A Guide to Maternity Leave and Maternity Pay' by Leah Waller
'The Queen's Counsel Lawyer's Omnibus: 20 Years of Cartoons from The Times 1993-2013' by Alex Steuart Williams

These books and more are available to order online direct from the publisher at www.lawbriefpublishing.com, where you can also read free sample chapters. For any queries, contact us on 0844 587 2383 or mail@lawbriefpublishing.com.

Our books are also usually in stock at www.amazon.co.uk with free next day delivery for Prime members, and at good legal bookshops such as Hammicks and Wildy & Sons.

We are regularly launching new books in our series of practical day-to-day practitioners' guides. Visit our website and join our free newsletter to be kept informed and to receive special offers, free chapters, etc.

You can also follow us on Twitter at www.twitter.com/lawbriefpub.

www.ingramcontent.com/pod-product-compliance
Lightning Source LLC
LaVergne TN
LVHW022112200926
848481LV00003B/1146
* 9 7 8 1 9 1 1 0 3 5 7 4 9 *